HTML, CSS, and DHTML
Frequently Asked Questions

Compiled by Terry Sanchez-Clark

HTML, CSS, and DHTML Frequently Asked Questions
978-1933804-61-0

compiled by Terry Sanchez-Clark
edited by Emilee Newman Bowles

Printed in the USA

Table of Contents

I. Introduction: HTML, CSS, & DHTML

This portion defines HTML, CSS, and DHTML. It also tackles a brief history of these topics.

II. HTML

> II.A. XHTML and Browser issues
>
> II.B. DIV issues
>
> II.C. Float issues and WMA file
>
> II.D. HTML elements

III. CSS

> III.A. Style Sheet printing problems
>
> III.B. Menu issues
>
> III.C. Technical issues

IV. HTML and CSS Combo

This portion tackles problems concerning both HTML and CSS.

V. DHTML

> V.A. Frequently asked questions about DHTML
>
> V.B. Events, Collections, Constants, Methods, Properties, and Objects defined by DHTML

In computing, **HyperText Markup Language** (**HTML**) is a markup language designed for the creation of web pages with hypertext and other information to be displayed in a web browser. HTML is used to structure information—denoting certain text as headings, paragraphs, lists and so on—and can be used to describe, to some degree, the appearance and semantics of a document. HTML's grammar structure is the HTML DTD that was created using SGML syntax.

Originally defined by Tim Berners-Lee and further developed by the IETF, HTML is now an international standard (ISO/IEC 15445:2000). Later HTML specifications are maintained by the World Wide Web Consortium (W3C).

Early versions of HTML were defined with looser syntactic rules which helped its adoption by those unfamiliar with web publishing. Web browsers commonly made assumptions about intent and proceeded with rendering of the page. Over time, the trend in the official standards has been to create an increasingly strict language syntax; however, browsers still continue to render pages that are far from valid HTML.

XHTML, which applies the stricter rules of XML to HTML to make it easier to process and maintain, is the W3C's successor to HTML. As such, many consider XHTML to be the current version of HTML, but it is a separate, parallel standard; the W3C continues to recommend the use of either XHTML 1.1, XHTML 1.0, or HTML 4.01 for web publishing.

In computing, **Cascading Style Sheets (CSS)** is a style sheet language used to describe the presentation of a document written in a markup language. Its most common application is to style web pages written in HTML and XHTML, but the language can be applied to any kind of XML document, including SVG and XUL. The CSS specifications are maintained by the World Wide Web Consortium (W3C). In order to maintain standards compliance, it is recommended that CSS code be validated before release.

CSS is used by both authors and readers of web pages to define colors, fonts, layout, and other aspects of document presentation. It is designed primarily to enable the separation of document content (written in HTML or a similar markup language) from document presentation (written in CSS). This separation can improve content accessibility, provide more flexibility and control in the specification of presentational characteristics, and reduce complexity and repetition in the structural content. CSS can also allow the same markup page to be presented in different styles for different rendering methods, such as on-screen, in print, by voice (when read out by a speech-based browser or screen reader) and on braille-based, tactile devices. Similarly, identical HTML or XML markup can be displayed in a variety of styles, brands, liveries or color schemes by using different CSS.

Style sheets have been around in one form or another since the beginning of SGML in the 1970s. Various browsers included their own style language which could be used to customize the appearance of web documents. Originally, style sheets were targeted towards the end-user; early revisions of HTML did not provide many facilities for presentational attributes, so it was often up to the browser to decide how web documents would appear.

As HTML grew, it came to encompass a wider variety of stylistic capabilities to meet the demands of web developers. This gave the designer more control over site appearance, but HTML became more complex to write and maintain. Variations in web browser implementations made consistent site appearance difficult and users had less control over their web browsing experience.

Seeing the need for an improved web presentation system, nine different style sheet languages were proposed to the W3C's www-style mailing list. Of the nine proposals, two were chosen as the foundation for what became CSS: Cascading HTML Style Sheets (CHSS) and Stream-based Style Sheet Proposal (SSP). First, Håkon Wium Lie (known today as the CTO of Opera Software) proposed Cascading HTML Style Sheets (CHSS) in October 1994, a language which has some resemblance to today's CSS. At that time, Bert Bos was working on a browser called Argo which used its own style sheet language (SSP). The two decided to work together (with the CSS Working Group) to develop CSS (the H was dropped when they realized that CSS could be applied to other markup languages too).

Unlike existing style languages like DSSSL and FOSI, CSS allowed a document's style to be influenced by multiple style sheets. One style sheet could inherit or "cascade" from another, permitting a mixture of stylistic preferences controlled equally by the site designer and user.

Håkon's proposal was presented at the "Mosaic and the Web" conference in Chicago, Illinois in 1994, and again with Bert Bos in 1995. Around this time, the World Wide Web Consortium was being established. The W3C took an interest in the development of CSS, and organized a workshop toward that end chaired by Steven Pemberton. This resulted in W3C adding work on CSS to the deliverables of the HTML editorial review board (ERB). Håkon and Bert were the primary technical staff on this aspect of the project with additional members, including Thomas Reardon of Microsoft, participating as well. By the end of 1996, CSS was ready to become official and the CSS level 1 Recommendation was published in December of that year.

Development of HTML, CSS, and the DOM had all been taking place in one group, the HTML Editorial Review Board (ERB). Early in 1997, the ERB was split into three working groups: the HTML Working group chaired by Dan Connolly of W3C, the DOM Working group chaired by Lauren Wood of SoftQuad, and the CSS Working group chaired by Chris Lilley of W3C.

The CSS Working Group began tackling issues that had not been addressed with CSS level 1, resulting in the creation of CSS level 2, with a first public Working Draft on November 4, 1997. It was published as a W3C Recommendation on May 12, 1998. CSS level 3, which was started in 1998, was still under development as of 2005.

Dynamic HTML or **DHTML** is a method of creating interactive web sites by using a combination of static markup language (such as HTML), a client-side scripting language (such as JavaScript), the presentation definition language (e.g., Cascading Style Sheets [CSS]), and the Document Object Model. Some disadvantages of DHTML are that it is difficult to develop and debug due to varying degrees of support among web browsers of the aforementioned technologies and that the variety of screen sizes means that the end look can only be fine-tuned on a limited number of browser and screen-size combinations. Development for recent browsers, such as Internet Explorer 5.0+, Netscape 6.0+, and Opera 7.0+, is aided by a shared Document Object Model.

Like LAMP, SPA, or Ajax, DHTML is not a technology in itself, but a term that refers to the use of a group of technologies together.

Though the term "dynamic web page" can refer to any specific web page that is generated differently for each user, load occurrence, or per specific variable values, those pages with this type of "dynamic" content should not be confused for DHTML. Web pages with this type of dynamic content, though still dynamic web pages, are a result of either server-side scripting (such as PHP), which generates unique content prior to sending the page to the visitor; or as a result of client-side scripting that is run immediately upon page load, before the static page content is visually generated. DHTML, as described above, is a term specifically reserved for those pages which utilize client-side scripting to effect changes in variables of the presentation definition language, which in turn affect the look and function of otherwise "static" HTML page content, *after* the page has been fully loaded and during the viewing process. In effect, the dynamic characteristic of DHTML is found in how it acts and functions as each page is being viewed, not in its ability to generate a unique page with each specific page load.

HTML, XHTML and Browser Issues

Question 1: Alternative to "onerror"

I need to use the "<img attribte onerror>" to load placeholder images on all dead image links, to get rid of my page with that awful missing "X" thumbnails. Unfortunately, "onerror" is not a valid XHTML transitional.

The images were uploaded on remote servers, so using a server side solution is not going to help.

As a result, my pages are not XHTML valid because of this one error.

What is the solution to this?

A: You can use a JavaScript function that loops through the DOM to get the image tags. Also, check their status and replace the SRC attribute accordingly.

Here's a quicker solution:

Code:

```
window.onload: function(){
    var imageList :  document.getElementsByTagName('IMG');
    var i;
    for(i: 0;i<imageList.length;i++){
        if(imageList[i].height <:  1){
            imageList[i].setAttribute('src','images/noImage
.gif');
        }
    }
}
```

Question 2: Firefox Ignores Colspan: "2"

I am inputting a table into a <TD> tag using AJAX and "td.id.innerHTML." The table displays fine but with <td colspan: "2"> the table will not span both columns. It worked perfectly in Internet Explorer. I can't figure out why only Firefox is ignoring it, I get no errors pertaining to the "colspan" in my JavaScript console.

This is the table row I am inserting into:

```
<tr id: "vinTablerow" style: "display: none">
    <td colspan: "2" id: "vinTable">
    </td>
    <td></td>
</tr>
```

I am using:

```
 document.getElementById("vinTable").innerHTML :   <TABLE
border: "1"><tr><tH>VIN</tH><TH>Phy Dmg
Symbol</TH><TH>Liability Symbol</TH><TH>ABS</TH><TH>Passive
Restraints</TH><TH>DRL</TH><TH>Performance
Type</TH><TH>Anti-Theft</TH><TH>MR Class</TH></tr><TR
ondblclick: "updateFormValues(event)" id: "row1"><TD id:
"vin">1234567890</TD><TD id: "damage">Physical
Damage</TD><TD id: "Liability">Liable</TD><TD id:
"ABS">YES</TD><TD id: "Restraint">Auto Seatbelt</TD><TD id:
"DRL">NO</TD><TD id: "performance">Exotic</TD><TD id:
"theft">Ignition Kill</TD><TD id: "MR">High
risk</TD></TR><TR  ondblclick: "updateFormValues(event)"
id: "row2"><TD id: "vin">0123456789</TD><TD id:
"damage">Dent</TD><TD id: "Liability">Not Liable</TD><TD
id: "ABS">NO</TD><TD id: "Restraint">Driver Side
Airbag</TD><TD id: "DRL">YES</TD><TD id:
"performance">Slow</TD><TD id: "theft">Alarm</TD><TD id:
"MR">medium risk</TD></TR></TABLE>
```

Then, switching the table row to:

```
dojo.byId("vinTablerow").style.display: "block";
dojo.byId is the same as getElementById
```

I have also tried the following:

```
<tr id: "vinTablerow" style: "display: none">
   <td colspan: "2" id: "vinTable">
   </td>
</tr>
```

Neither seems to make a difference.

Is there a way to fix this?

A: All I can say is that FireFox has absolutely no problems with applying "colspan" or "rowspan."

As a possible error, default display for table row is "table-row" and not "block." Your shifting from "table-row" to "none to block" could confuse FF, which is stricter in these rules than IE. Try to change the "innerHTML" without switching the display of the row.

Question 3: Positioning with XHTML

I used the following code to position items when I using regular HTML code, but now I'm upgrading my skills to XHTML and this code no longer works.

Here's an example:

```
<img src: "top.jpg" div style: "position: absolute; top:0;
left:0">
```

I will use the same "div style: etc." to position everything from graphics to tables and, even my "iframes." Why isn't it working in XHTML? How can I make it work?

A: You should align the image in the top left corner.

```
Code:
```

```
<img src: "top.jpg" style: "position:absolute; top:0px;
left:0px">
```

Whatever that div was in your code, it was completely erroneous, either in HTML or XHTML. Style tag launches CSS and positions the element via CSS. The same can be achieved through the style sheet in the head of the document or best in a separate file.

However, I have found that maintaining a site that is fully absolutely positioned can be a nightmare (since you have to reposition everything if you decide to add something or lengthen the other thing), and I advise people to use the normal document flow whenever possible.

If using XHTML, you should also terminate your "img" element:

```
Code:
```

```
<img ... />
```

Question 4: Error displaying page in FireFox

I'm using Visual Studio 2003 (C#) to create a simple ASPX login page.

The following is the layout of the page:

```
------------------------------
|  User:        Passwd:       |
|                             |
------------------------------
```

I have the following in pseudo code:

```
<div with top of frame image> </div>
<div with side of frame image>
   <form>User, Passwd...</form>
</div>
<div with bottom of frame image></div>
```

After I built the project and ra n it in Internet Explorer, everything worked perfectly. But when I run the same page with Firefox that I get the following:

```
------------------------------
|                            |
------------------------------
     User:     Passwd:
```

I don't understand why it doesn't respect the DIVS in FireFox.

Here's the HTML Code:

```
<%@ Page language: "c#" Codebehind: "Default.aspx.cs"
AutoEventWireup: "false" Inherits: "JudgeReports.WebForm1"
%>
<!DOCTYPE HTML PUBLIC "-//W3C//DTD HTML 4.0
Transitional//EN" >
<HTML>
    <HEAD>
        <title>Judge Reports</title>
        <meta content: "Microsoft Visual Studio .NET 7.1"
name: "GENERATOR">
        <meta content: "C#" name: "CODE_LANGUAGE">
        <meta content: "JavaScript" name:
"vs_defaultClientScript">
        <meta content:
"http://schemas.microsoft.com/intellisense/ie5" name:
"vs_targetSchema">
        <LINK href: "StyleSheet1.css" type: "text/css" rel:
"stylesheet">
    </HEAD>
    <body ms_positioning: "GridLayout">
        <h1 align: "center">Judge Reports Login Page</h1>
        <div class: "top-frame"></div>
        <div class: "side-frame">
            <form id: "Form1" method: "post" runat: "server">
                <div class: "login">
                    <br>
                    <asp:Label Runat: "server" id:
"lblUser">User:</asp:Label>
                    <asp:TextBox Runat: "server" ID:
"txbUser"></asp:TextBox>
                    <asp:Label Runat: "server" id:
"lblPassword">    Password:</asp:Label>
                    <asp:TextBox Runat: "server" ID:
"txbPassword" TextMode: "Password"></asp:TextBox>
                        
                    <asp:Button Runat: "server" ID:
"btnLogin" Text: "Login"></asp:Button>
                    <br>
                    <br>
                    <asp:RequiredFieldValidator Runat:
"server" ID: "rfvUser" ControlToValidate: "txbUser"
ErrorMessage: "User
Required!!!"></asp:RequiredFieldValidator>
                    <asp:RequiredFieldValidator Runat:
"server" ID: "rfvPassword" ControlToValidate: "txbPassword"
ErrorMessage: "    Password
Required!!!"></asp:RequiredFieldValidator>
                    <asp:Label Runat: "server" ID:
"lblError" ForeColor: "red"></asp:Label>
                </div>
            </form>
        </div>
```

22

```
        <div class: "bottom-frame"></div>
    </body>
</HTML>

Style Sheet:

body
{
    text-align: center;
}

.top-frame
{
    width: 750px;
    height: 7px;
    background-image: url(Images/TopFrame.gif);
    background-repeat: no-repeat;
    background-position: bottom;
    padding-top: 5px;
    padding-bottom: 5px;
}

.bottom-frame
{
    width: 750px;
    height: 7px;
    background-image: url(Images/BottomFrame.gif);
    background-repeat: no-repeat;
    background-position: top;
    padding-top: 5px;
    padding-bottom: 5px;
}

.side-frame
{
    width: 750px;
    height: 3px;
    background-image: url(Images/SideFrame.gif);
    background-repeat: repeat;
}

.login
{
    padding-left:10px;
    padding-right:10px;
    padding-top:10px;
}
```

After I load the page
(http://localhost/JudgeReports/Default.aspx) and then
view the source, this is what I get with Internet Explorer:

Code:

```
<!DOCTYPE HTML PUBLIC "-//W3C//DTD HTML 4.0
Transitional//EN" >
<HTML>
    <HEAD>
        <title>Judge Reports</title>
        <meta content: "Microsoft Visual Studio .NET 7.1"
name: "GENERATOR">
        <meta content: "C#" name: "CODE_LANGUAGE">
        <meta content: "JavaScript" name:
"vs_defaultClientScript">
        <meta content:
"http://schemas.microsoft.com/intellisense/ie5" name:
"vs_targetSchema">
        <LINK href: "StyleSheet1.css" type: "text/css" rel:
"stylesheet">
    </HEAD>
    <body ms_positioning: "GridLayout">
        <h1 align: "center">Judge Reports Login Page</h1>
        <div class: "top-frame"></div>
        <div class: "side-frame">
            <form name: "Form1" method: "post" action:
"Default.aspx" language: "javascript" onsubmit: "if
(!ValidatorOnSubmit()) return false;" id: "Form1">
<input type: "hidden" name: "__VIEWSTATE" value:
"dDwxNDA1NTI2OTI7Oz7qIIOpybO6bhtYECT4EqWN4b2XBw:  : " />

<script language: "javascript" type: "text/javascript" src:
"/aspnet_client/system_web/1_1_4322/WebUIValidation.js"></s
cript>

                <div class: "login">
                    <br>
                    <span id: "lblUser">User:</span>
                    <input name: "txbUser" type: "text" id:
"txbUser" />
                    <span id:
"lblPassword">    Password:</span>
                    <input name: "txbPassword" type:
"password" id: "txbPassword" />
                        
                    <input type: "submit" name: "btnLogin"
value: "Login" onclick: "if (typeof(Page_ClientValidate) :
:  'function') Page_ClientValidate(); " language:
"javascript" id: "btnLogin" />
                    <br>
                    <br>
                    <span id: "rfvUser" controltovalidate:
"txbUser" errormessage: "User Required!!!"
evaluationfunction: "RequiredFieldValidatorEvaluateIsValid"
initialvalue: "" style: "color:Red;visibility:hidden;">User
Required!!!</span>
                    <span id: "rfvPassword"
controltovalidate: "txbPassword" errormessage:
```

24

```
"     Password Required!!!" evaluationfunction:
"RequiredFieldValidatorEvaluateIsValid" initialvalue: ""
style: "color:Red;visibility:hidden;">     Password
Required!!!</span>
                    <span id: "lblError" style:
"color:Red;"></span>
               </div>

<script language: "javascript" type: "text/javascript">
<!--
    var Page_Validators :    new
Array(document.all["rfvUser"],
document.all["rfvPassword"]);
        // -->
</script>


<script language: "javascript" type: "text/javascript">
<!--
var Page_ValidationActive :   false;
if (typeof(clientInformation) !:   "undefined" &&
clientInformation.appName.indexOf("Explorer") !:   -1) {
    if (typeof(Page_ValidationVer) : :   "undefined")
        alert("Unable to find script library
'/aspnet_client/system_web/1_1_4322/WebUIValidation.js'.
Try placing this file manually, or reinstall by running
'aspnet_regiis -c'.");
    else if (Page_ValidationVer !:   "125")
        alert("This page uses an incorrect version of
WebUIValidation.js. The page expects version 125. The
script library is " + Page_ValidationVer + ".");
    else
        ValidatorOnLoad();
}

function ValidatorOnSubmit() {
    if (Page_ValidationActive) {
        return ValidatorCommonOnSubmit();
    }
    return true;
}
// -->
</script>



        </form>
        </div>
        <div class: "bottom-frame"></div>
    </body>
</HTML>
```

With Firefox:

```
<!DOCTYPE HTML PUBLIC "-//W3C//DTD HTML 4.0
Transitional//EN" >
<HTML>
    <HEAD>
        <title>Judge Reports</title>
        <meta content: "Microsoft Visual Studio .NET 7.1"
name: "GENERATOR">
        <meta content: "C#" name: "CODE_LANGUAGE">
        <meta content: "JavaScript" name:
"vs_defaultClientScript">
        <meta content:
"http://schemas.microsoft.com/intellisense/ie5" name:
"vs_targetSchema">
        <LINK href: "StyleSheet1.css" type: "text/css" rel:
"stylesheet">

    </HEAD>
    <body ms_positioning: "GridLayout">
        <h1 align: "center">Judge Reports Login Page</h1>
        <div class: "top-frame"></div>
        <div class: "side-frame">
            <form name: "Form1" method: "post" action:
"Default.aspx" id: "Form1">
<input type: "hidden" name: "__VIEWSTATE" value:
"dDwxNDA1NTI2OTI7Oz7qIIOpybO6bhtYECT4EqWN4b2XBw: : " />

                <div class: "login">

                    <br>
                    <span id: "lblUser">User:</span>
                    <input name: "txbUser" type: "text" id:
"txbUser" />
                    <span id:
"lblPassword">    Password:</span>
                    <input name: "txbPassword" type:
"password" id: "txbPassword" />
                        
                    <input type: "submit" name: "btnLogin"
value: "Login" onclick: "if (typeof(Page_ClientValidate) :
: 'function') Page_ClientValidate(); " language:
"javascript" id: "btnLogin" />
                    <br>

                    <br>
                     
                     
                    <span id: "lblError"><font color:
"Red"></font></span>
                </div>
            </form>
        </div>
        <div class: "bottom-frame"></div>
    </body>
```

```
</HTML>
```

What could be the solution for this problem?

A: You can try taking the height: "3px;" line out of ".side-frame" in your style sheet. This affects the layout of your images and text.

DIV Issues

Question 5: Force Wordwrap Inside <div></div>

How can I force word wrap inside "<div id: "mydiv" style: "width: 55"></div>" after I dynamically change its visibility?

```
document.getElementById( 'mydiv' ).style.display :   'none';
document.getElementById( 'mydiv' ).style.display :   '';
```

It seems that dynamically changing the display ruins the width property. This was tested on Firefox only.

A: Check how you are changing the style. Maybe it's more than just with the display property. Check if your "myDiv" is really a div.

DIVS are block elements by default.

Try to display "block" instead of ".

You can also check out the white-space and word-wrap CSS properties.

Question 6: Divs Allowed within Object Tags

This is the where you can find the validation report:

http://validator.w3.org/check?uri:
www.liessem.no%2FArbeidsmappe%2Findex.php

Quoted from the site:

The document located at
<http://www.liessem.no/Arbeidsmappe/index.php> was
checked and found to be valid HTML 4.01 Strict. This
means that the resource in question identified itself as
"HTML 4.01 Strict" and that we successfully performed a
formal validation using an SGML or XML Parser
(depending on the markup language used).
To show your readers that you have taken the care to create
an interoperable Web page, you may display this icon on
any page that validates. Here is the HTML you could use to
add this icon to your Web page:

```
<p>
   <a href: "http://validator.w3.org/check?uri:
referer"><img
        src: "http://www.w3.org/Icons/valid-html401"
        alt: "Valid HTML 4.01 Strict" height: "31" width:
"88"></a>
   </p>
```

If you like, you can download a copy of this image (in PNG
or GIF format) to keep in your local web directory, and
change the HTML fragment above to reference your local
image rather than the one on this server.
If you use CSS in your document, you should also check it
for validity using the W3C CSS Validation Service.
If you would like to create a link to *this* page (i.e., this
validation result) to make it easier to revalidate this page in
the future or to allow others to validate your page, the URI
is <http://validator.w3.org/check?uri:
http%3A%2F%2Fwww.liessem.no%2FArbeidsmappe%2Fi
ndex.php> (or you can just add the current page to your
bookmarks or hotlist).

The W3C Validator Team

This is the site:
http://www.liessem.no/Arbeidsmappe/index.php

DIVS allowed within object tags seems to be the only thing that causes the site I'm working on not to validate. Why is this?

A: Try to do what the validator report' suggests.

First, put all that in a div. Apparently, object cannot be a direct child of "noscript."

It's true what the validator says. You are closing a div that's never been opened, at least that's what the source shows. Count the divs. Proper code indentation helps fix problems like these.

You can also try putting the object in its very own div.

Question 7: "Clear: left" is Forcing Next div onto New Line

I have four DIVS. I want two of them to appear on one line and the other two on the next line, right underneath each other. I've set it clear: left on the third div so that it goes into a new line, but the following happens as a result:

1. It decreases the left margin.

2. It forces the fourth div onto a new line instead of putting it beside the third one.

I also tried putting clear: right on the second div which gives the desired effect, except it increases the left margin on the second div.

This is a link to the site:

http://www.doghousebooks.ie/doghouse/authors.php

This is a print screen of the site:

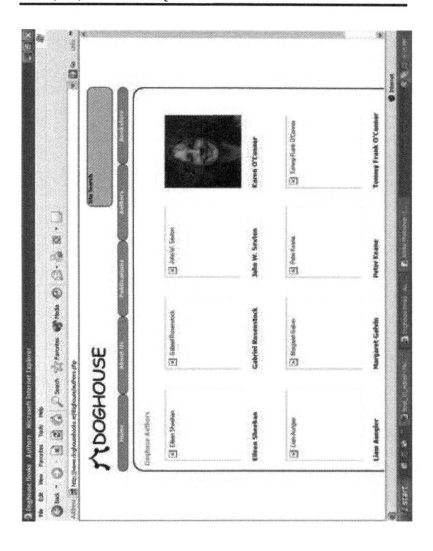

The larger DIV in the middle is where I tried using "clear: left" on the third div. The smaller ones at the bottom are where I put "clear: right" on the second div.

How can I resolve this problem?

A: First, your main content borders are overlapping the menu, use "clear: both;" on "#main_tl" to fix that.

Second, to achieve the two divs side to side in the first line, do "float: left" on both of them. To do the same on the second line, you omit the "float: left" for the first three div in the second line. Just float both in the second line as well and you'll be better off. From there, you're more or less set. I believe the bigger margin appears in IE because of a known hack regarding double margins and floats. Again, if you float everything, you will get rid of that problem.

I suppose you don't need the second set of smaller boxes and they were there just for presentation. They looked completely messed up in Mozilla.

It's not fun to do debugging for IE, because it is so unpredictable and the only thing I can think of is adding another element to do the clear. This would be best done with a horizontal rule stuck between the two groups. It's not a perfect solution, but it works:

Code:

```
<div id: "one" style: "float: left; margin-left: 10px;
background-color: #ff9900; width: 90px; height:
90px">one</div>
<div id: "two" style: "float: left; margin-left: 10px;
background-color: #ff0000; width: 90px; height:
90px">two</div>
<hr style: "visibility: hidden; clear: both;" />
<div id: "three" style: "float: left; margin-top: 10px;
margin-left: 10px; width: 90px; height: 90px; background-
color: #ff9900">three</div>
<div id: "four" style: "float: left; margin-top: 10px;
margin-left: 10px; width: 90px; height: 90px; background-
color: #ff0000">four</div>
```

Question 8: Forcing a DIV onto the Next Line

I have a div which is 800px long and contains 7 divs. 6 of the div's (3 top and 3 bottoms) from the top and bottom to give me rounded corners and work perfectly. However, at some point I want to "slide" another div in besides, (using JavaScript) and therefore need them to resize accordingly. This all worked fine, as long as none of the div's on the next "line" fits into the space on the right hand side. But obviously, as soon as the divs are small enough, it fits into the first available space (which I don't want them to do). I tried "clear: both" but that didn't do anything.

I tried to click the link at the bottom. As soon as I did, the "main_bl" div moves to the very top underneath the navigation bar.

Why did the W3C said that there is no language attribute (for the script tag) when I validated? If I don't put in the language attribute, how will the browsers know if I'm using JavaScript or another scripting language like jscript, etc.?

A: You can remove "float: left;" from "#main_body," and you can achieve the expected look and suffer no penalties for it.

The validator complains about the language attribute because script element has no language attribute. It does, however, have type attribute where you define the type. For your case, it would be: type: "text/javascript."
The content is centered in IE because it accepts the incorrect method of centering via "text-align: center;" method on your body tag. Text-align center should only work on text and not on block level elements. To center those, one needs to add "margin: 0 auto;" to their declaration. This means that the element should have a top and bottom margin of 0 and a left and right margin of auto. It means left and right should equally distribute any

remaining space in the width, thus shoving the element in the center. So, if you apply that "margin: 0 auto;" styles to your two main divs, that holds the entire page (the "#main_content" and the one that holds the navigation and header) and your page should be at the center. Adding "clear: both;" to the paragraph that holds the "make me smaller" will help it move to the bottom of the page.

Script tag language is identified by the type attribute.

Question 9: Explorer: 3px Margin for the IMG

I would like div box after (vertically) an image, but explorer will always insert a 3px margin between the "img" and the box.

Is it possible to get rid of it without needing table layout?

Here is what I have:

```
<img src: "img/box_about.gif" alt: "" />
<div class: "box">
    <p class: "title_box">Tharuka</p>
    <p class: "text_box">Reisefuhrerir</p>
</div>
```

A: That looks like the IE is incorrectly applying white space as actual space. Try making the "img" a block level element, or just try removing all the white space (new lines, spaces) between the <img> and the <div>.

Float Issues and WMA File

Question 10: Floats are Different across Browsers

IE is showing the "LEFTSIDE" and "RIGHTSIDE" as columns that are the entire height of the "middle" column.

Firefox is showing the middle column "wrap" around the "LEFTSIDE" and "RIGHTSIDE" columns.

Is there a solution for this?

A: Make the widths fixed so it doesn't get clipped. The height is already in there. You can try the following:

```
Code:
#leftside {
    FLOAT: left; WIDTH: 170px; HEIGHT: 100%;
    border:solid;
    border-color:red;

}
#rightside {
    FLOAT: right; WIDTH: 170px; HEIGHT: 100%
}
#middle {
    width:500px;
    FLOAT: left;
    border:solid;
}
```

Question 11: Floating link – Scroll Bar

I have a div floating to the bottom and right side of the page. I have an image inside the div and it has a link on it. I used the following:

```
Code:
<div style: "right:0px; bottom:0px; width:141px;
height:141px; position:absolute;"><a href: "shows.php"><img
src: "img/nextshow.gif" width: "141" height: "141" border:
"0" /></a></div>
```

The problem occurs with FireFox. When you click the link, the scroll bars appear moving the link slightly up and to the left and sometimes even causing the "click" action to not go through and the user must click again to follow the link. If the link didn't work the first time and if you click off away from the div (like in some blank space), the scroll bars goes away.

How can I fix this?

A: You can try to substitute "position: absolute;" with "position: fixed;" for most modern browsers to work the way you want. IE 6.0, however, does not support this and you will need to employ JavaScript for IE.

Incidentally, if you want to get rid of the dotted border around the links in FF, you can use "outline: none;" on the links you want to remove it from.

Question 12: Left Float is Floating Right

I presume the problem is something to do with nesting, but I can't see where this DIV is inheriting the "float: right" setting from. Here's the body of my code (it does validate as strict xhtml 1.1):

```
Code:
<body style: "text-align: center">

<div style: "width: 800px; border: 0px; text-align: left">
<div style: "width: 100%; height: 60px">
<img src: "images/logo.jpg" alt: "Logo" style: "float:
left" />
<div id: "search"><b>  Site Search</b></div>
</div>

<div class: "nav"><div class: "left"></div><div class:
"right"></div><a href: "/home.php" class:
"nav">Home</a></div>
<div class: "nav"><div class: "left"></div><div class:
"right"></div><a href: "about-us.php" class: "nav">About
Us</a></div>
<div class: "nav"><div class: "left"></div><div class:
"right"></div><a href: "publications.php" class:
"nav">Publications</a></div>
<div class: "nav"><div class: "left"></div><div class:
"right"></div><a href: "authors.php" class:
"nav">Authors</a></div>
<div class: "nav"><div class: "left"></div><div class:
"right"></div><a href: "shop.php" class:
"nav">Bookstore</a></div>
<br><br>

<div style: "height: 20px; width: 20px; background:
url(images/main_tl.jpg); float: left"> </div><div
style: "width: 760px; height: 20px; border-top: 2px solid
#002E71; float: left"> </div><div style: "height:
20px; width: 20px; background: url(images/main_tr.jpg);
float: right"> </div>

<div style: "height: 20px; width: 20px; background:
url(images/main_bl.jpg); float: left"> </div><div
style: "width: 760px; height: 20px; border-top: 2px solid
#002E71; float: left"> </div><div style: "height:
20px; width: 20px; background: url(images/main_br.jpg);
float: right"> </div>

</div>
</body>
```

It's the second set of DIVs that's causing the problem. The div with background "main_bl" floats to the right for some reason. Then, the next div is forced onto the next line with the next div beside it. Why didn't they line up like the three before them? The strange thing I've noticed is, if I put more content in that DIV (the one that keeps floating right) it then floats to the left correctly, but only if there are enough characters for the background to repeat.

Do you have any idea on how to fix this?

A: After the first set of divs, clear the content by using "clear: both;" either with a new element or with a div starting the next batch.

Your problem happens because of the way float works. Since your float process is uninterrupted, the first of the second group of divs looks for the highest (page-wise) position it can float in. For some reason, your last div in the first row is smaller in height than the first two. So, the next div lodges there. If you clear the floats, next div will float under the longest div of the first batch.

This is speculation though because I can't really see how the website looks like, but the problem you're mentioning points to that.

I'll stick with my explanation. The width of the div plays a part as well. 20px can cram underneath the third div, but 21px can't. I don't see the page, nor know which browser you use, so it is hard to say why this happens. But it looks more and more to be the issue of the fourth div getting into the first available spot to float, and that is all the way to the right. The clearing solution would be the most correct one, so you shouldn't feel bad about using it. It just says something like: "this is a new line, begin floating elements anew."

I suggest you use the tested and tried method described here:

http://www.alistapart.com/articles/customcorners/

The design

...decide on some basic layout parameters...

Step 1.1 shows how we slice up the sketch.

Note: Obviously, you can use any element to hook graphics up with. Your document's markup is unlikely to exactly match the structure used in our example. For all we know, you may only have a single paragraph of text to which you hope to apply customized corners and borders. You can easily do so.

As stated earlier, all you need is at least four structural elements. (Depending on the height of your element you may require five.) If necessary, these elements could be nonsemantic divs, each with its own class. Just remember that for a div element to be rendered, it must contain content to manifest its presence. Also keep in mind that if your content lends itself to common structural elements such as headers, paragraphs, and so on, you can and should use those instead of relying on nonsemantic divs.

The styles
To continue, let's turn on element borders and set a relative width for the div that contains the whole article, to see how things behave:

```
div.Article {
  width:35%;
  border: 1px solid red; }
div.Article h2 {
  border: 1px solid blue; }
div.ArticleBody {
  border: 1px solid black; }
div.ArticleFooter {
  border: 1px solid blue; }
```

```
div.ArticleFooter p {
  border: 1px solid magenta; }
 See Step 2 — basic element behaviour
```

Nothing really surprising here. We do, however, take notice of the gaps appearing before and after our div class: "ArticleBody." Ignoring that problem for now, we'll go on and write ourselves a style sheet:

```
body {
  background: #cbdea8;
  font: 0.7em/1.5 Geneva, Arial, Helvetica, sans-serif;
  }
div.Article {
  background:
       url(images/custom_corners_topleft.gif)
  top left no-repeat;
  width:35%;
  }
div.Article h2 {
  background:
       url(images/custom_corners_topright.gif)
  top right no-repeat;
  }
div.ArticleBody {
  background:
       url(images/custom_corners_rightborder.gif)
  top right repeat-y;
  }
div.ArticleFooter {
  background:
       url(images/custom_corners_bottomleft.gif)
  bottom left no-repeat;
  }
div.ArticleFooter p {
  background:
       url(images/custom_corners_bottomright.gif)
  bottom right no-repeat;
  }
See Step 3 — first attempt
```

Not bad at all! Actually better than we expected. Obviously we need to add some padding to our respective elements to make the layout look better — and then there are those pesky gaps to fix. The gaps are caused by the carriage returns inserted by our paragraph (block) elements. We could avoid using paragraph elements altogether and thereby bypass the problem, but — for reasons well-known to ALA readers — we prefer to keep our markup structurally clean and logical. It isn't our data's fault that we are lazy stylers.

In our first pass, we assumed that a carriage return must equal 1.5em, as that was the value we specified for our line-height. Therefore our first attempt was to add a margin-top:-1.5em to our ArticleBody and ArticleFooter. It worked perfectly in most standards-compatible browsers — all except the ones used by the 94% of internet users on this planet (no names, please).

After testing, trial, error, rinse, and repeat we find that we must use at least a margin-top:-2em to be sure that the elements touch and the gap closes:

```
div.Article {
  background:
       url(images/custom_corners_topleft.gif)
  top left no-repeat;
  width:35%;
  }
div.Article h2 {
  background:
       url(images/custom_corners_topright.gif)
  top right no-repeat;
  font-size:1.3em;
  padding:15px;
  margin:0;
  }
div.ArticleBody {
  background:
       url(images/custom_corners_rightborder.gif)
  top right repeat-y;
  margin:0;
  margin-top:-2em;
  padding:15px;
  }
div.ArticleFooter {
  background:
       url(images/custom_corners_bottomleft.gif)
  bottom left no-repeat;
  }
div.ArticleFooter p {
  background:
       url(images/custom_corners_bottomright.gif)
  bottom right no-repeat;
  display:block;
  padding:15px;
  margin:-2em 0 0 0;
```

```
}
```

Question 13: Embedding a WMA File

After eight years in the business of web design, I'm
embarrassed to say that I really don't know how to embed a
WMA file without the controls. I've tried the following but
I get an error:

IN THE HEAD:

```
<script>

}

function MM_controlSound(x, _sndObj, sndFile) { //v3.0
var i, method : "", sndObj : eval(_sndObj);
if (sndObj !: null) {
if (navigator.appName : : 'Netscape') method : "play";
else {
if (window.MM_WMP : : null) {
window.MM_WMP : false;
for(i in sndObj) if (i : : "ActiveMovie") {
window.MM_WMP : true; break;
} }
if (window.MM_WMP) method : "play";
else if (sndObj.FileName) method : "run";
} }
if (method) eval(_sndObj+"."+method+"()");
else window.location : sndFile;
}
//-->
</script>
```

THE BOTTOM OF PAGE:

```
<object data: "/audio/coldblue.wma" codetype: "audio/x-ms-
wma"> </object>
<embed name: 'CS1091944428707' src: '/audio/coldblue.wma'
loop: "False"
autostart: "True" mastersound hidden: "True" width: "0"
height: "0"></embed>
```

The above code gives me an Unsafe Active X control
message.

Why does this happen?

A: Typing "embed wma without controls" into Google
gives this as the first hit:

http://www.jakeludington.com/project_studio/20051015
_embedding_windows_media_player_wma.html

Notice they have a "showControls" parameter set to true.
Perhaps, you can set this to false.

To quote:

When you offer a direct download, users click on a link to
the audio file and either view the video in their desktop
Windows Media Player or save it to their hard drive. To
stream your audio file with visible Windows Media Player
controls, you need to embed the player in the page where
you post your audio file. This requires some specific HTML
code included in the page or blog post where the audio is
linked.

There are some potential headaches to this method,
including support for browsers like Firefox and Safari. Mac
users don't have Windows Media Player installed by
default and Safari issues a nasty warning message with no
link to the resolution on Macs without Windows Media
Player. Internet Explorer handles embedded Windows
Media files nicely, which is to be expected since it's also a
Microsoft product. For broad compatibility with all
browsers, it's best to stick with the version 6.4 embedded
player (which has nothing to do with the version of desktop
player the user might have installed).

There are certain things every embedded Windows Media
Player needs to function properly, along with a long list of
optional parameters. Each embedded player instance on
your Web page needs the object definition to clarify which
version of the Windows Media Player will be called. This is
identified by both the CLSID reference and the CODEBASE
definition. For the 6.4 version of the embedded player this
looks like the example below:

```
<object id: "MediaPlayer" height: 46 classid:
"CLSID:22D6f312-B0F6-11D0-94AB-0080C74C7E95" standby:
"Loading Windows Media Player components..." type:
"application/x-oleobject" codebase:
"http://activex.microsoft.com/activex/controls/mplayer/en/n
smp2inf.cab#Version: 6,4,7,1112">
```

The one required parameter is the location of your audio file, which is defined using the "filename" parameter:

```
<param name: "filename" value:
"http://yourdomain/youraudio.mp3">
```

Some optional parameters include showing the Windows Media Player controls and whether the audio starts automatically. Since you are using the Showcontrols parameter, keep in mind your player height should be 46 pixels to accommodate the height of the files. The height parameter isn't required, but leaving it out causes the player to resize as it's loading, creating an ugly experience for your listener.

```
<param name: "Showcontrols" value: "True">
<param name: "autoStart" value: "True">
```

The final part of the implementation is the embed statement which includes the application you are embedding and a link to your video file like this:

```
<embed type: "application/x-mplayer2" src: "
http://yourdomain.com/youraudio.mp3" name: "MediaPlayer"
width: 320 height: 240></embed>
```

The finished code looks like the example below, which you can copy for your own site and simply replace the links to your audio file where appropriate and adjust the necessary height settings.

```
<object id: "MediaPlayer" height: 46 classid:
"CLSID:22D6f312-B0F6-11D0-94AB-0080C74C7E95" standby:
"Loading Windows Media Player components..." type:
"application/x-oleobject" codebase:
"http://activex.microsoft.com/activex/controls/mplayer/en/n
smp2inf.cab#Version: 6,4,7,1112">
```

```
<param name: "filename" value:
"http://yourdomain.com/youraudio.mp3">
<param name: "Showcontrols" value: "True">
<param name: "autoStart" value: "True">

<embed type: "application/x-mplayer2" src: "
http://yourdomain.com/youraudio.mp3" name:
"MediaPlayer"></embed>

</object>
```

HTML Elements

Question 14: Gap under image

I have the following:

```
Code:
#container {
    text-align: center;
}
#body {
    width: 750px;
    border: 1px solid #006699;
    margin-right:auto;
    margin-left:auto;
    overflow: auto;
}
#menu {
    margin-left: auto;
    margin-right: auto;
    background-color: #6179B5;
    border-top: 1px solid #CCCCCC;
    color: white;
    font-family:verdana;
    font-size: 12px;
    padding: 2px;
}
#content {
    text-align: left;
    padding: 10px;
}
#footer {
    clear: both;
}
```

Why is IE putting a gap below the header graphic?

A: It looks like it might be a white space issue. Try removing all your tabs and line breaks. If it fixes the issue, put them back in one at a time until you find the offending one(s).

Once found, you can get around the issue by splitting your closing ">" to the next line, for example:

```
Code:
    <sometag ... some attributes ... />
</someothertag>
```

becomes this:

```
Code:
   <sometag ... some attributes ...
/></someothertag>
```

Question 15: Setting Row Span

I am generating an HTML table from an SQL query with PHP. One of my table columns contains a picture. The column row is spanned in accordingly.

However, my records come back from the database. I tried giving the hard coded "rowspan" a crazy, much higher number of rows that were in the table.

It did not produce an error, but is this okay?

A: Yes it is okay, but not very standard. You can use a PHP function to get the number of records returned. I think it's "mysql_num_rows()," and then just set the "rowspan" using that number.

Question 16: Background Color - Alpha

How can I apply a transparency to a background color?

A: You can try this:

http://www.mandarindesign.com/opacity.html

A warning is in order—it may or may not work on all browsers yet and it may produce unexpected behaviors on some browsers.

Question 17: Background Not Showing In

I've got a web page that has a background color specified on the body, and contains a TD tag with an image as a background (<td border: "1" background: "events....jpg">). The browser is IE 6.0. AOL is installed.

I've got a user complaining that they can't see the image. The body's background is white (not the expected color) and the text is also a different font than what I specified.

Why is this one user having a problem?

A: Without a valid HTML, there's no telling what unique things will occur with your pages when users make use of different browsers.

Some things to fix and keep in mind are:

- Always add a Doctype
- Always make sure you have the appropriate HTML code (HTML, HEAD, BODY, etc. tags)

You can set up a user defined style sheet by going to Tools/Internet Options and in the General tab, choose Accessibility. The last item on that window is to add a custom style sheet.

However, your page is not valid HTML. I'd bet if you work through those issues first, the browser output would solve itself more easily.

Question 18: Link Doesn't Show the Right Color

I can't get my link to post the color I want. You can view it here:

http://www.dlfmedia.com/events.html_

I have two links in the content section that I want to be "#FFCC00," instead they are displaying the same color as the <p> so you can't distinguish that it's a link. I tried enclosing it in a <span>, and I tried adding a class to my <a>. Both showed up "#FFCC00" in Dreamweaver, but when I preview it in a browser it is still the same color as the <p>.

How can I resolve my problem?

A: It looks fine in both IE6/Win and FX1.5.0.2/Win.

Check if you're looking at a cached version or a temp file. Check the URL and clear your cache.

Holding shift and clicking the refresh button will also pull all fresh data from the server, ensuring nothing on the page is cached.

Question 19: Font Trickery - Extending the "Standard" Collection

I have a page and I want to enable the user to utilize more than the few available standard web fonts.

Is there some hack to have, say, a collection of 20 custom TrueType fonts that a user can *transparently* download just by viewing the page?

A: To embed a font type on a WebPage first select the font you want to embed either from your hard drive or download it from the Internet. Then create an embedded font file (below). And lastly, attach the font to your style sheet.

1. Creating the Embedded File. You need to download software to create an embedded font file which can be in two formats:

```
.pfr   or   .eot.
```

2. Portable Font Resources (.pfr): TrueDoc for Nav 4.0+ and IE 4.0+ on Windows, Mac, and Unix platforms. Download the software from http://Bitstream.com.

3. Embeddable Open Type (.eot): Compatible only with Explorer 4.0+ on the Windows platform. Download the software from
```
http://www.microsoft.com/typography/web/embedding/weft3/def
ault.htm.
```
4. Next we need to embed the file using CSS. This can be done 2 ways:

Both are placed into the HEAD section of your document insert:

Example with True Doc:

```
<link rel: "fontdef" src: "my-fancy-font.pfr">
```

To work in IE4 and above, you need to add a pointer to an ActiveX control immediately after the LINK tag or the easier option: create an OpenType file for Explorer and refer to both types on your page.

TrueDoc fonts stay within the browser: you can't download them to your system.

Example with Open Type:

```
<STYLE TYPE: "text/css">
<--!
@font-face {
    src:url(myfonts/fontname.eot);
}
-->
</STYLE>
```

Question 20: Disable an Input Element but Still Have Black Text

I want the element to look normal, but not be editable.

Do I have to trap keystrokes for this?

A: Try setting the "readonly" property:

Code:

```
<input type: "text" readonly: "readonly" value: "try to
type over me" />
```

Question 21: Match Text with Google Ads

How can I match text and links with Google ads?

http://www.spyderscripts.com/ads/ads.html

The top one is the ad, the rest are my links and text I want to match identically. I can't put my finger on it, but the fonts or the sizes between their ads and my text are not identical.

Are they using a different font? Is there a different size?

Also, why did my links have a gap between the link and the underline? I've never had that happen before.

A: You are using a completely different font to the Google ad. They are using sans-serif fonts (Verdana); you are using serif fonts (Times New Roman).

The serif is the "twiddly" bit on the ends of the characters. Sans-serif fonts don't have these.

The Google ad appears inside an <iframe>. If you want to view what is going on you can right click on it and then select "This Frame > View Frame Source." The Google code is pretty terrible (<font> elements used as <span>s FFS!), but the appropriate part is:
Code:

```
<font style: "font-size:11px; font-
family:verdana,arial,sans-serif; line-height:14px;">
<a class: "ad" id: "aw0" target: "_top" href:
"/pagead/iclk?sa: l&ai: BuV ... etc ..." onFocus: "ss('go
to www.TShirtStudio.com','aw0')" onClick: "ha('aw0')"
onMouseOver: "return ss('go to
www.TShirtStudio.com','aw0')"  onMouseOut: "cs()">
<b>Design your own Jigsaws</b></a></font>
```

Question 22: Margin Problems IE vs FF

I'm trying to get some boxes to appear in the same place on both IE and FF, but I'm having some difficulty doing so. Try to check it on the following site:

http://test.referee-assistant.com/index_css2.php

Take a look at the gray box on the left and the green box on the right. I basically want the edges of both boxes to line up with the interior edge of the simulated drop-shadow graphic on their respective side of the page.

What can I do to get consistent results? Or is this something I'll just need to live with?

A: You can edit the margin style in the "div#more" rule from this:

```
Code: margin: 0 20px 0 0;
```

To this:

```
Code:
margin: 0 20px 0 0;
_margin-right: 0px;
```

If that works, and you want your CSS to validate, then you can include the "_margin property" in an IE CSS, linked in with conditional comments, etc.

Also try to change "`_margin: 0px`" to "`_display:inline.`"

If it fixes it, run with it. If not, revert to the original fix.

Question 23: Exit a Text Box when Enter is Pressed

How can I create a text box that executes a function when the user presses the ENTER key?

I'm an experienced programmer (VB/VFP), but can't seem to get a handle on the oriented structure.

I've looked around for the form but can't find it.

What book would you recommend for JavaScript commands, references, and functions, etc.?

A: If by text box you mean text area, the enter key will result in a new line.

If by text box you mean text input box, then the enter key will execute default action in a form. You can probably work with the "onsubmit" event handler then.

You can try the "onkeypress" event and then fire a "subfunction" based on the key press value.

I threw this together as an example:

```
Code:

<html>
<head>
<script type: "text/javascript">
function lolEvent(event)
{
event.keyCode : :  13 ? alert("lol") : alert("notlol");
}

</script>
</head>

<body>
<form>

Press enter to make me lol:
```

```
<input type: "text" onkeyPress: "lolEvent(event)">
</form>

</body>

</html>
```

Question 24: Multi Line Textbox not Wrapping in Firefox

I have a .NET multi line textbox that I have set to wrap and not scroll horizontally. It works great in IE, but in Firefox it just keeps scrolling. I was thinking it must be an easy fix, but I have not found it yet.

This is the client-side code that is generated by the .net control:

```
<Asp:Textbox id: "descr" CssClass: "fborder" Runat: "server"
TextMode: "MultiLine" Wrap: True Width: "70%" Height: "150"
/>
```

And here is the rendered HTML in Firefox:

```
<textarea name: "descr" id: "descr" class: "fborder" style:
"height:150px;width:70%;"></textarea>
```

The behavior in IE is that it wraps with no horizontal scroll bars period. With Firefox, it will only wrap at a break.

So, is it possible to make it behave in Firefox as it does in IE?

A: No, it's not possible. While IE supports the word-break CSS property, FF has nothing similar to work with. A long string of text without breaks will always stay in one line in FF.

Question 25: Input Box on Form Losing Focus

I have a form which has dynamically populated dropdowns. There is also an input box that needs to be filled in before submission.

Now, the problem is that in Firefox I can't get the input box to keep its focus. In IE, everything is fine. But when I click in the box in FF, the focus switched back to the dropdown bow above.

Here is the code:

Code:

```
<form action: "villasearch.php" method: "post" name:
"proprent" id: "proprent" onsubmit:
"YY_checkform('proprent','Bedrooms','#q','1','Number of
Bedrooms must be selected');return
document.MM_returnValue">
      <label> <br />
        <span class: "formspacing">
          <?
          echo "<select name: 'country' onchange:
\"reload(this.form)\" class: \"formelements\"><option
value: '' >Country?</option>";
while($noticia2 :  mysql_fetch_array($quer2)) {
if($noticia2['cid']: : @$country){echo "<option selected
value:
'$noticia2[cid]'>$noticia2[country_name]</option>"."<BR>";}
else{echo  "<option value:
'$noticia2[cid]'>$noticia2[country_name]</option>";}
}
echo "</select>";
?>
        </span><br />
        <br />
        </label>
      <label>
        <?
        echo "<select name: 'region' class:
\"formelements\"><option value: ''>Region?</option>";
while($noticia :  mysql_fetch_array($quer)) {
echo  "<option value:
'$noticia[rid]'>$noticia[region_name]</option>";
}
```

```
echo "</select>";
?>
        <br />
        <br />
        <input name: "beds" class: "formelements" id:
"beds" onFocus: "if(this.value: : 'Bedrooms?')this.value:
'';" value: "Bedrooms?"/>

        </label>
     <br />
     <br />
     <div align: "right">
        <label>
           <input type: "submit" name: "Submit" value:
"Submit" />
        </label>
     </div>
     </form>
```

Here is the client side form code:

```
<form action: "villasearch.php" method: "post" name:
"proprent" id: "proprent" onsubmit:
"YY_checkform('proprent','Bedrooms','#q','1','Number of
Bedrooms must be selected');return
document.MM_returnValue">
        <label> <br />
        <span class: "formspacing">

           <select name: 'country' onchange:
"reload(this.form)" class: "formelements"><option value: ''
>Country?</option><option value:
'1'>Australia</option><option selected value:
'14'>England</option><BR></select>          </span><br />
        <br />
        </label>
     <label>
        <select name: 'region' class:
"formelements"><option value: ''>Region?</option><option
value: '52'>Norfolk</option><option value:
'58'>Yorkshire</option></select>          <br />

        <br />
        <input name: "beds" class: "formelements" id:
"beds" onFocus: "if(this.value: : 'Bedrooms?')this.value:
'';" value: "Bedrooms?"/>

        </label>
     <br />
     <br />
     <div align: "right">
        <label>
           <input type: "submit" name: "Submit" value:
```

```
"Submit" />
        </label>

    </div>
    </form>
```

And the JavaScript codes, both validated and reloaded have these for the dropdowns:

```
function YY_checkform() { //v4.71
//copyright (c)1998,2002 Yaromat.com
  var a: YY_checkform.arguments,oo: true,v: '',s: '',err:
false,r,o,at,o1,t,i,j,ma,rx,cd,cm,cy,dte,at;
  for (i: 1; i<a.length;i: i+4){
    if (a[i+1].charAt(0): : '#'){r: true; a[i+1]:
a[i+1].substring(1);}else{r: false}
    o: MM_findObj(a[i].replace(/\[\d+\]/ig,""));
    o1: MM_findObj(a[i+1].replace(/\[\d+\]/ig,""));
    v: o.value;t: a[i+2];
    if (o.type: : 'text'||o.type: : 'password'||o.type: :
'hidden'){
      if (r&&v.length: : 0){err: true}
      if (v.length>0)
      if (t: : 1){ //fromto
        ma: a[i+1].split('_');if(isNaN(v)||v<ma[0]/1||v >
ma[1]/1){err: true}
      } else if (t: : 2){
        rx: new RegExp("^[\\w\.: -]+@[\\w\\.-]+\\.[a-zA-
Z]{2,4}$");if(!rx.test(v))err: true;
      } else if (t: : 3){ // date
        ma: a[i+1].split("#");at: v.match(ma[0]);
        if(at){
          cd: (at[ma[1]])?at[ma[1]]:1;cm: at[ma[2]]-1;cy:
at[ma[3]];
          dte: new Date(cy,cm,cd);
          if(dte.getFullYear()!: cy||dte.getDate()!:
cd||dte.getMonth()!: cm){err: true};
        }else{err: true}
      } else if (t: : 4){ // time
        ma: a[i+1].split("#");at:
v.match(ma[0]);if(!at){err: true}
      } else if (t: : 5){ // check this 2
          if(o1.length)o1:
o1[a[i+1].replace(/(.*\[)|(\].*)/ig,"")];
          if(!o1.checked){err: true}
      } else if (t: : 6){ // the same
          if(v!: MM_findObj(a[i+1]).value){err: true}
      }
    } else
    if (!o.type&&o.length>0&&o[0].type: : 'radio'){
        at :  a[i].match(/(.*)\[(\d+)\].*/i);
        o2: (o.length>1)?o[at[2]]:o;
      if (t: : 1&&o2&&o2.checked&&o1&&o1.value.length/1: :
```

```
0){err: true}
     if (t: : 2){
       oo: false;
       for(j: 0;j<o.length;j++){oo: oo||o[j].checked}
       if(!oo){s+: '* '+a[i+3]+'\n'}
     }
   } else if (o.type: : 'checkbox'){
     if((t: : 1&&o.checked: : false)||(t: :
2&&o.checked&&o1&&o1.value.length/1: : 0)){err: true}
   } else if (o.type: : 'select-one'||o.type: : 'select-
multiple'){
     if(t: : 1&&o.selectedIndex/1: : 0){err: true}
   }else if (o.type: : 'textarea'){
     if(v.length<a[i+1]){err: true}
   }
   if (err){s+: '* '+a[i+3]+'\n'; err: false}
  }
  if (s!: ''){alert('You have not fully filled in the
form.:\t\t\t\t\n\n'+s)}
  document.MM_returnValue :  (s: : '');
}
//-->

function reload(form){
var val:
form.country.options[form.country.options.selectedIndex].va
lue;
self.location: 'index.php?country: ' + val ;

}
```

It might be worth mentioning that I have two forms on this page. The second form is virtually identical to the first; it just looks at a different table to get the options and the reload JavaScript is replaced by:

```
function reloaded(form){
var val:
form.country1.options[form.country1.options.selectedIndex].
value;
self.location: 'index.php?country1: ' + val ;

}
```

What am I doing wrong here?

A: Check the label tag you have. It might be messed up and relating virtually everything to the region box in the form. Try to strip them if you think you don't need them anywhere.

You could also consider cutting down the validation function to just the bare essentials. That looks like a generic "do-it-all" function, which you probably don't need.

If you use the code on other pages, then you should probably leave it as is. After all, if it works, why change it?

If it was only on the one page, then you could cut it down considerably.

Question 26: Z-index of Form Elements

I have a drop down menu and have placed a select list just below it. I've tried playing with the z-index but cannot seem to get the menu to drop over the select list.

How can I resolve this problem?

A: Unfortunately, this is an unresolved issue. All the browsers are having problems with this so you might want to rethink the design of your drop down menu.

This unresolved issue can be further referenced from the IE, Firefox, and Netscape websites—if you want to do further research. You may also want to go and check this out:

http://www.webreference.com/dhtml/diner/seethru/

There is a glimmer of hope though. There's an alternative to fix it in IE7. If your menu is flash, that might also make a difference.

You can consult the following websites for specific alternatives:

http://tanny.ica.com/ica/tko/tkoblog.nsf/dx/select-tag-overlap-in-ie-part-ii

http://tanny.ica.com/ica/tko/tkoblog.nsf/dx/Select-tag-overlap-in-IE

http://homepage.mac.com/igstudio/design/ulsmenus/vertical-uls-iframe.html

Question 27: Z-Index is Fine in IE but Disappeared in FireFox

I used a "z-index:-1" for one of my images, it shows up as it is intended to in IE. But in FireFox, the image disappeared.

How can I fix this?

A: Don't use "-1." I think FireFox (correctly) places negative indexes behind the body, and therefore they can't be seen.

The picture is clearly behind everything else, say HTML element which has z-index of 0. So, your image cannot be seen. Try using positive values and just give your other elements a higher z-index.

Question 28: Fit Graphic to Window

If I set a link to open in a new window, can I make the size of the window fit the graphics?

For example, a 6" graphic contained within a 6" window so you don't see the dead space.

A: You cannot set window widths in inches, you can only specify pixels.

You can use:

```
<a href: "imageFilename.jpg" onclick:
"void(window.open(this.href, '', 'width: 600,height:
400')); return(false);">Click here</a>
```

"Void" simply stops the return value being passed back to the page.

"return (false)" stops the anchor opening the original image. Users without JavaScript will still see the image, though.

To move the window to a certain location, add "left: n,top: n" to the 3rd parameter in the open call.

Question 29: Fitting a Table within a Frame

I've created a table in HTML that centers itself horizontally on the page. However, I understand that frames size themselves according to the fraction the page that the frame takes up.

Is there a way to have a table fit within a frame regardless of the resolution of the user? I'm pretty sure that I won't be able to account for every user, but I would like that so that the frame would size itself around the table and no scrolling need to occur.

A: This mainly depends on the table you're putting in your frame and the resolutions you want to support. Fitting 20 columns into 640px is nearly impossible.

That said, you can have the frame resized after the content has loaded to fit the content size via JavaScript. You can also just include the table in the main page. If you will just resize the frame the page it is in, you can make it look like there's no frame at all.

Question 30: Frame Problems in IE7

Obviously, IE7 is still beta, so I don't have to officially support it yet. But some of my clients are early adopter types, which spells trouble on the way. In a nutshell, I manage a real time reporting system for my company that delivers data to clients via Web pages. It's built on an ASP.net back end, with some other stuff tossed in for good confusion. I didn't design the core.

The main pages use a NavBar style frameset where the top frame contains a toolbar with buttons for the various pages a client might have, and the lower frame contains the data page. I used the <base target> tag for the links in the navigation bar to force them to load in the lower frame.

Recently, I downloaded IE7 on my personal machine just to check it out and on a whim hit my work site just to see how it displayed. Unfortunately, that was a bad thing. What I get in IE7 is the initial frameset builds, but when the links are selected, data loads in the top navbar frame rather than the lower data frame.

I've dug around and haven't found anything specific on IE7 changing or dropping support for the old frameset tags. Generally, I don't go for frames, but several of these clients go back a few years and for a while, this navbar approach has been the standard. That said, at the current time, I don't really have the manpower to go back and revamp several hundred pages to completely remove or change the frame coding, so I'm desperately trying to find out what's happening with IE7 to see if there's an easy fix.

Is anyone playing with IE7 yet and if so, have you worked with frames at all?

A: Here is the link to the Microsoft's Knowledge Base article regarding the Base Element:

http://msdn.microsoft.com/workshop/author/dhtml/refer
ence/objects/base.asp

Directly quoted, here is the content:

BASE Element | base Object

Specifies an explicit URL used to resolve links and
references to external sources such as images and style
sheets.

Members Table

The following table lists the members exposed by the base
object. Click a tab on the left to choose the type of member
you want to view.

The following table lists the members exposed by the **base**
object. Click a tab on the left to choose the type of member
you want to view.

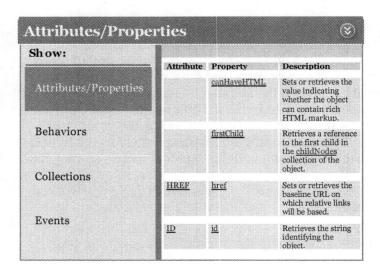

Methods		isContentEditable	Retrieves the value indicating whether the user can edit the contents of the object.
Styles		isDisabled	Retrieves the value indicating whether the user can interact with the object.
		isMultiLine	Retrieves the value indicating whether the content of the object contains one or more lines.
		isTextEdit	Retrieves whether a TextRange object can be created using the object.
		lastChild	Retrieves a reference to the last child in the **childNodes** collection of an object.
		nextSibling	Retrieves a reference to the next child of the parent for the object.
		nodeName	Retrieves the name of a particular type of node.
		nodeType	Retrieves the type of the requested node.
		nodeValue	Sets or retrieves the value of a node.
		ownerDocument	Retrieves the document object associated with the node.
		parentElement	Retrieves the parent object in the object hierarchy.
		parentNode	Retrieves the parent object in the document hierarchy.
		parentTextEdit	Retrieves the container object in the document hierarchy that can be used to create a **TextRange** containing the original object.
		previousSibling	Retrieves a reference to the previous child of the parent for the object.

	readyState	Retrieves the current state of the object.
	scopeName	Retrieves the namespace defined for the element.
	sourceIndex	Retrieves the ordinal position of the object, in source order, as the object appears in the document's all collection.
	tagName	Retrieves the tag name of the object.
	tagUrn	Sets or retrieves the Uniform Resource Name (URN) specified in the namespace declaration.
TARGET	target	Sets or retrieves the window or frame at which to target content.
	uniqueID	Retrieves an autogenerated, unique identifier for the object.

Behavior	Description
clientCaps	Provides information about features supported by Microsoft Internet Explorer, as well as a way for installing browser components on demand.
download	Downloads a file and notifies a specified callback function when the download is complete.
homePage	Contains information about a user's homepage.

Collection	Description
all	Returns a reference to the collection of elements contained by the object.
attributes	Retrieves a collection of attributes of the object.
behaviorUrns	Returns a collection of Uniform Resource Name (URN) strings identifying the behaviors attached to the element.
childNodes	Retrieves a collection of HTML Elements and TextNode objects that are direct descendants of the specified object.
children	Retrieves a collection of DHTML Objects that are direct

descendants of the object.

Event	Description
onlayoutcomplete	Fires when the print or print preview layout process finishes filling the current LayoutRect object with content from the source document.
onmouseenter	Fires when the user moves the mouse pointer into the object.
onmouseleave	Fires when the user moves the mouse pointer outside the boundaries of the object.
onreadystatechange	Fires when the state of the object has changed.

Method	Description
addBehavior	Attaches a behavior to the element.
applyElement	Makes the element either a child or parent of another element.
attachEvent	Binds the specified function to an event, so that the function gets called whenever the event fires on the object.
clearAttributes	Removes all attributes and values from the object.
cloneNode	Copies a reference to the object from the document hierarchy.
componentFromPoint	Returns the component located at the specified coordinates via certain events.
contains	Checks whether the given element is contained within the object.
detachEvent	Unbinds the specified function from the event, so that the function stops receiving notifications when the event fires.
fireEvent	Fires a specified event on the object.
getAdjacentText	Returns the adjacent text string.
getAttribute	Retrieves the value of the specified attribute.
getAttributeNode	Retrieves an attribute object referenced by the **attribute.**name property.
getBoundingClientRect	Retrieves an object that specifies the bounds of a collection of TextRectangle objects.
getClientRects	Retrieves a collection of rectangles that describes the layout of the contents of an object or range

	within the client. Each rectangle describes a single line.
getElementsByTagName	Retrieves a collection of objects based on the specified element name.
hasChildNodes	Returns a value that indicates whether the object has children.
insertAdjacentElement	Inserts an element at the specified location.
mergeAttributes	Copies all read/write attributes to the specified element.
normalize	Merges adjacent **TextNode** objects to produce a normalized document object model.
removeAttribute	Removes the given attribute from the object.
removeAttributeNode	Removes an **attribute** object from the object.
removeBehavior	Detaches a **behavior** from the element.
replaceAdjacentText	Replaces the text adjacent to the element.
setAttribute	Sets the value of the specified attribute.
setAttributeNode	Sets an **attribute** object node as part of the object.
swapNode	Exchanges the location of two objects in the document hierarchy.

Style attribute	Style property	Description
background-position -x	backgroundPositionX	Sets or retrieves the x -coordinate of the backgroundPosition property.
background-position -y	backgroundPositionY	Sets or retrieves the y -coordinate of the **backgroundPosition** property.
behavior	behavior	Sets or retrieves the location of the **Dynamic HTML (DHTML) behavior**.
layout-grid	layoutGrid	Sets or retrieves the composite document grid properties that specify the layout of text characters.
layout-grid-mode	layoutGridMode	Sets or retrieves whether the text layout grid uses two dimensions.
	pixelBottom	Sets or retrieves the bottom position of the object.
	pixelHeight	Sets or retrieves the height of the object.

	pixelLeft	Sets or retrieves the left position of the object.
	pixelRight	Sets or retrieves the right position of the object.
	pixelTop	Sets or retrieves the top position of the object.
	pixelWidth	Sets or retrieves the width of the object.
	posBottom	Sets or retrieves the bottom position of the object in the units specified by the bottom attribute.
	posHeight	Sets or retrieves the height of the object in the units specified by the height attribute.
	posLeft	Sets or retrieves the left position of the object in the units specified by the left attribute.
	posRight	Sets or retrieves the right position of the object in the units specified by the right attribute.
	posTop	Sets or retrieves the top position of the object in the units specified by the top attribute.
	posWidth	Sets or retrieves the width of the object in the units specified by the width attribute.
text-autospace	textAutospace	Sets or retrieves the autospacing and narrow space width adjustment of text.
text-underline-position	textUnderlinePosition	Sets or retrieves the position of the underline decoration that is set through the textDecoration property of the object.

Remarks:

When used, the base element must appear within the head of the document, before any elements that refer to an external source.

Note: Versions of Internet Explorer prior to Windows Internet Explorer 7 would allow the base element to appear anywhere in the document tree, which caused relative paths to use the "nearest" base element as the base for the URL. Internet Explorer 7 strictly enforces the use of the base tag within the head of the document, and will ignore misplaced tags.

If more than one base element occurs, only the first element will be recognized.

This element is not rendered.

This element does not require a closing tag.

Examples

This example sets the base URL of the document to a reference folder. Internet Explorer uses the base element to resolve the link to:

http://msdn.microsoft.com/workshop/author/dhtml/reference/properties/href_2.asp.

```
<html>
<head>
  <base href:
"http://msdn.microsoft.com/workshop/author/dhtml/reference/
"/>
</head>

<body>
Click <a href: "properties/href_2.asp">here</a> to learn
about the
href property.
</body>
</html>
```

This example retrieves the base URL from the document if a valid base element is specified in the document. Otherwise, the function returns null.

```
<script>
function GetBase()
```

```
{
    var oBaseColl :  document.all.tags('BASE');
    return ( (oBaseColl && oBaseColl.length) ?
oBaseColl[0].href :
        null );
}
</script>
Standards Information
```

This object is defined in HTML 3.2.

Question 31: "seamless" Iframe or Regular Frames

I'm trying to load different contents in the bottom half of my page based on a menu click in the top half of my page. But I want them to appear as one seamless page and the background images need to line up perfectly. All the options I've tried for the frames have left me with a noticeable space between frames or an indented box where the iframe is.

Is there a way that I can accomplish this?

A: You can try the following code:

```
<html>
<head>

<style type: "text/css">
<!--
iframe   {
    border: 0px;
    margin: 0px;
    padding:  0px;
}

#frame1 {
    display:block;
    width:  100%;
}

#frame2 {
```

```
    display:block;
    width:  100%;
}
-->
</style>

</head>
<body>
<iframe id: "frame1" src: "http://google.com"></iframe>
<iframe id: "frame2" src: "http://google.com"></iframe>
</body>
</html>
```

You can also add the following:

```
<html>
<head>

<style type: "text/css">
<!--
iframe   {
    border: 0px;
    margin: 0px;
    padding:  0px;
}

#frame1 {
    display:block;
    width:  100%;
}

#frame2 {
    display:block;
    width:  100%;
}
-->
</style>

</head>
<body bgcolor: "#5C5D60">
<iframe id: "frame1" src: "http://google.com" frameborder:
"0" marginheight: "0"></iframe>
<iframe id: "frame2" src: "http://google.com" frameborder:
"0" marginheight: "0"></iframe>
</body>
</html>
```

Question 32: Mouse Handler Inserts Gap Below Image

I have a navigation bar with a series of images stacked in the cells of a table. "Onmouseover" and "onmouseout" swaps images. I keep ending up with a gap between the images in two of the cells.

This is all I'm doing:

Code:

```
<a href: "about_us.htm">
<img border: "0" onmouseover: "document.contactButton.src:
'imgs/e_contact_u.gif'" onclick:
"document.contactButton.src: 'imgs/e_contact_d.gif'"
onmouseout: "document.contactButton.src:
'imgs/e_contact.gif'" src: "imgs/e_contact.gif" name:
"contactButton" width: "165" height: "90">
```

You can check out this link and tell me what I'm doing wrong:

http://www.thedarcygroup.com/xindex.htm

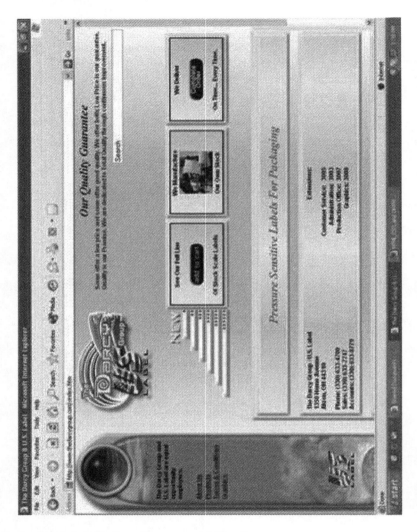

Is there a solution for my problem?

A: What I see right away is that you have a load of white space. Try removing it all and see if that helps.

You can try to change a portion of your code from this:

```
<td width: "165" height: "90" valign: "bottom">
<a href: "about_us.htm">
<img border: "0" onmouseover: "document.contactButton.src:
'imgs/e_contact_u.gif'" onclick:
"document.contactButton.src: 'imgs/e_contact_d.gif'"
onmouseout: "document.contactButton.src:
'imgs/e_contact.gif'" src: "imgs/e_contact.gif" name:
"contactButton" width: "165" height: "90">
</a>
    </td>
```

To a version without white space:

```
<td width: "165" height: "90" valign: "bottom"><a href:
"about_us.htm"><img border: "0" onmouseover:
"document.contactButton.src: 'imgs/e_contact_u.gif'"
onclick: "document.contactButton.src:
'imgs/e_contact_d.gif'" onmouseout:
"document.contactButton.src: 'imgs/e_contact.gif'" src:
"imgs/e_contact.gif" name: "contactButton" width: "165"
height: "90"></a></td>
```

This way, you can also make it work in Mozilla.

Question 33: Containers

I have been using this JavaScript to round the corners and give the same height to the main content area with pictures and to the bios of the designers. I just noticed that the containers are no longer the same height, they are slightly off. Why does this occur?

Only the home page on the main navigation bar has a page and Metal "Pointu subnav" under jewelry too.

The other problems that still need fixing are as follows:

1. I used a <br> tag after the second image to force two images per line. I know I should use CSS for this but I don't know how.

2. I also know the JS for light boxes is causing the shaking images.

3. I've got my padding and margins on my nav and subnav items to line up on the left side, but it was through sheer trial and error. Is there a better way to do it?

I wanted my main nav items slightly spaced out, but that made it hard to align the subnav items. My only requirements are that they align on the left with a little space between them and the edge, and that they are spaced out a little.

How can I fix these problems?

A: Your #content is 492px wide. Your "#tablecontentcontainer" which resides inside the 492px #content has a width of 490px plus 5px padding on each side and 10px left margin, making it effectively occupy the space of 510px. While stuffing 510px element into 492px one, FF just hangs it over and IE expands the parent container to 510px. So, change the properties to whatever you desire of "#tablecontentcontainer" so that its entire width (width, margin, padding and borders) will be less or equal to 492px.

As for the rest, I see no problems in Mozilla or IE6.

Other than that, your main container is actually 760px wide (750px width + 10px for padding), so your effective area is 750px.

Question 34: IE 7 quick-wins

I installed IE 7 Beta 2 this morning to test our site, and have a few "quick-wins" which developers may find handy.

The underscore hack no longer works. This involved prefixing style properties with an underscore to make them IE-only, such as " _display:inline;" etc. If I like to use this sort of thing, I can replace the underscore with an asterisk (e.g., *display:inline;), which will work in IE 7 as well as in earlier versions.

IE 7 supports min-width and min-height. Therefore, if I patch width or height for IE, my sites will break in IE 7. If I use the underscore hack, I'm safe. I have things like this:

Code:

```
<style type: "text/css">
    someEl {
        min-height: 200px;
        _height: 200px;
    }
</style>
```

It works fine in IE 7, as it ignores the height rule. However, if I did not use the underscore hack (for validation reasons), settling for conditional comments instead:

```
<style type: "text/css">
    someEl {
        min-height: 200px;
    }
</style>
<!--[if IE]>
<style type: "text/css">
    someEl {
        height: 200px;
    }
</style>
<![endif]-->
```

Then, I will have to specifically exclude IE 7:

Code:

```
<style type: "text/css">
    someEl {
        min-height: 200px;
    }
</style>
<!--[if lt IE 7]>
<style type: "text/css">
    someEl {
        height: 200px;
    }
</style>
<![endif]-->
```

Please take note that all of the above was working on HTML 4.01 Strict DOCTYPE. I cannot say how the information will work with regards to other DOCTYPES.

How can I modify it?

A: My understanding is that they've fixed the * html hack too, so this will have the desired effect and also validate:

Code:

```
<style type: "text/css">
    someEl {
        min-height: 200px; /* moderns inc. IE7 */
    }

    * html someEl {
        height: 200px;   /* IE6 and lower */
```

```
    }
</style>
```

Unlike conditional comments, you can use this technique in your external style sheets too.

For an article on the bug-fixes in IE7, you can refer to the following URL:

http://www.devarticles.com/c/a/Web-Style-Sheets/CSS-Standards-Compliance-in-Internet-Explorer-7/

This is helpful if you use a lot of IE6 hacks.

Question 35: <...> Proprietary Attribute "..."

I have this tag:

<html XMLNS:t: "urn:schemas-microsoft-com:time"
xmlns:v: "urn:schemas-microsoft-com:vml>

Can it be used with FF?

I'm guessing it's not due to the Microsoft part, but how can I know for sure?

Is there a fix for this?

A: Unfortunately, there is no fix for this. This is Microsoft's (HTML+TIME) "Timed Interactive Multimedia Extensions" which is used for adding timing and media synchronization support to HTML pages.

Question 36: Selected Menu

I have a horizontal drop down menu on the top of my page.

How can I indicate that a menu has been selected? For example, I want to highlight the menu I have selected.

A: The body id is a technique for highlighting the current page's entry in a menu. You give each page in your site a different id, and a matching class in the menu, like this:

```
Code:
<body id: "home">
<h1>Home Page</h1>
<ul>
<li class: "home"><a href: "/">Home</a></li>
<li class: "about"><a href: "about.htm">About</a></li>
</ul>
</body>
<body id: "about">
<h1>About Us</h1>
<ul>
<li class: "home"><a href: "/">Home</a></li>
<li class: "about"><a href: "about.htm">About</a></li>
</ul>
</body>
```

Then, you can put this in your style sheet:

```
Code:
#home .home,
#about .about {
    color: red;
}
```

Personally, I prefer to use SSI to build the menu dynamically, including a class: "current" in the current menu item. However, if that technique is not available to you, this one works pretty well.

Question 37: Light Box Pop-ups Not Working

My image on the home page is a link and it opens when you click on it but without the fancy box etc. You can see my errors at:

http://www.jean-jacquesgallery.com/storesite2

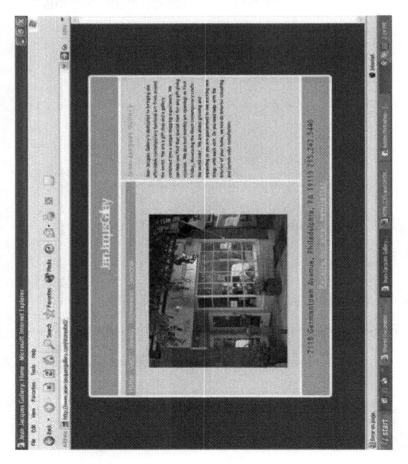

Only the Home page and the Metal Point page in the jewelry links are working. The photo on the Home page is the one I tried to apply the light box to. It wasn't resized, I wanted to try it out and I thought it would have all the effects and not just the resize. Maybe this causes the problem. It also has the blue box around it like an image link usually does. This leads me to believe I haven't applied the light box stuff correctly. I'm still playing around with the design and colors.

How can I solve make everything work and show correctly?

A: The problem is the path to your JavaScript:

```
Code:
<script type: "text/javascript" src:
"js/prototype.js"></script>
<script type: "text/javascript" src:
"js/scriptaculous.js?load: effects"></script>
```

The locations to prototype and scriptaculous are wrong.

If you have Web Developer toolbar for Firefox, you can go to:

```
"Information > View JavaScript"
```

You can get a 404 "not found" error for each of these scripts.

Question 38: Side Bar

On a website, usually there are links down the left hand side of a page. I was wondering if there is a way where I could place links down the side of the page. But if I need to change them, I would only have to change one page without changing others, preferably not using frames.

Is this possible?

A: You could use templates if you use a program such as frontpage or dreamweaver. If you use PHP, you can use a PHP include file.

If you have an external JavaScript (.js) file, you can use "document.writeln("")" here.

For example, in the html file:

```
<script SRC: "myMenu.js">
</script>
```

And in the file:

```
<!-- hide script from old browsers

document.writeln("<a href: "#">Option 1</a><br>");
document.writeln("<a href: "#">Option 2</a><br>");

// end hiding script from old browsers -->
```

You can also use server side includes. Have a look at this link with several URL that have easy to do tutorials:

http://www.google.com/search?hl: en&q: server+side+include&btnG: Google+Search

Question 39: Printing Background Color

Is there a way to have a background color print out on a printer?

A: Yes, there is a way.

Most browsers default to having background colours and images switched off when printing. Nevertheless, you'll probably want to suppress the background for the body element in your print stylesheet. If the user's browser is set to print backgrounds, your action will save on ink cartridges and make printing faster and your users will thank you for these things.

My testing shows that the following browsers not only suppress the body background by default but also the backgrounds of div, table, td and p elements (and presumably all other elements):- Opera (O7.54); Gecko (NS7.1: Gecko 1.4 and Firefox 1.0: Gecko 1.7.5); IE (5.0 and 6). The suppression, as part of the document's rendering, is controlled by the browser (albeit as a user preference). However, it can't be overridden through an author stylesheet. Instead, it is equivalent to the following rule in a user stylesheet (see UserStylesheets):-

```
@media print {
  * {
  background-color: white !important;
  background-image: none !important;
  }
}
```

This drastic suppression doesn't take the design of an individual Web document into account and can play havoc with its readability and general presentation. Since most users will have this browser setting (probably without knowing it) you may wish to take account of it in your Print Stylesheet and try to mitigate any damage.

Interestingly, Opera also suppresses borders set on div, table, td, and p elements (and presumably on all other elements).

I have also found that all the above browsers, in addition to suppressing backgrounds, may change text colours to black to try to ensure readability (for example, if a document has white text on a black background). Thus, your document may be printed very differently from how you intended.

Cascading Style Sheets:

Style Sheet Printing Problems

Question 40: Print Style Sheet—Doesn't Hide Elements Properly

I set up a print style sheet to hide my header and side menu, it's something like this:

```
#NavTop {display:none; }
```

But instead of hiding my header and side menu completely, it left a white blank space where my header and side menu used to be. It's like the header and menus are still there, but they are all white.

I am sure I have "display:none;" instead of "visibility:hidden;" my code looks something like this:

```
<div id: "NavTop">
<span class: "links">links</span>
</div>

<div id: "NavLeft">
<span class: "linksleft">linksleft</span>
</div>

<div id: "maincontent">
<span class: "content">Contents</span>
</div>
```

In my print style sheet, I put:

```
#NavTop {display:none; }
#NavLeft {display:none; }
```

How I can fix this?

A: The feature "display none" causes the element not to be displayed at all. What you are describing is behavior of "visibility:hidden."

From what was posted, I can only guess that something else is formatting your divs. The white space maybe caused by an absolutely position div, margin, or padding, etc.

By all means, you can use "position:absolute" on your display CSS, but your print CSS needs to have different margins and / or use different "absolute positioning."

An "absolute position" would explain the white space. You can try floating elements inside a div. It's hard to understand exactly what you are trying to accomplish without seeing the source code for your page or a working example. Anyway, look at this example. It will explain why the white space is showing up even when you do not display some divs.

http://www.w3schools.com/css/tryit.asp?filename: trycss_position_absolute

```
Code:

<html>
<head>
<style type: "text/css">
h2.pos_abs
{
position:absolute;
left:100px;
top:150px
}
</style>
</head>

<body>
<h2 class: "pos_abs">This is a heading with an absolute
position</h2>
<p>With absolute positioning, an element can be placed
anywhere on a page. The heading below is placed 100px from
the left of the page and 150px from the top of the
page.</p>
</body>

</html>
```

It looks like this:

With absolute positioning, an element can be placed anywhere on a page. The heading below is placed 100px from the left of the page and 150px from the top of the page.

This is a heading with an absolute position

Also, if it is a print style sheet, then you can probably just change the position attributes and reposition everything.

This is a great site to get the basics down:

http://www.w3schools.com/css/css_positioning.asp

you can just remove the positioning (no position absolute or value). Just erase all the positioning for your print CSS, and when you use "display:none" the white space will not be there. I haven't seen your layout, so while this may work it will also remove positioning (formatting) and you may need your document to look pretty.

Question 41: Checking Style Sheet

I am validating my style sheet with the w3 schools validator. I can get it to validate, but I have numerous warning tagged onto the end of it.

For example:

Line : 49 (Level : 2) font-family: You are encouraged to offer a generic family as a last alternative :

It is a last alternative to what? I have it set to my preferred font of Verdana, but whatever I put in there, I get this error. How can I fix this?

A: You should always specify a generic font family when your choice of font is not available. In your case, it would be "sans-serif":

Code:

```
font-family: Verdana, sans-serif;
```

Question 42: Printing Bar Graphs

I have a list of bar graphs that are dynamically created and I want to insure that they are not cut off during printing.

How can I make sure the graphs are printed in whole?

A: If you are dealing with CSS2, you can add page breaks like this:

```
<div style: "page-break-after: always"></div>
```

This will not work with some of the older browsers.

Question 43: Table Printing Tips

I have this nice form that I've developed. I programmed my CSS to re-format everything for printing. Everything fits the way it's supposed to. IE6 is the browser in use.

But on some of the tables, I have shaded backgrounds. Like where it says "Client Info," it's all shaded with nice grey all the way across the page, as a separator.

I want to be able to print that shaded background.

Now, keeping in mind that this form will be used on probably 2000 computers, turning on "print background images" isn't an option. It has to fly as it is.

Is there any way to override that as a 40% grey graphic overlay? Maybe someone has figured out a way to shade the background of a table cell when printing.

A: You can specify a border within each cell and that will show up when printing.

Example:

```
border: 1px solid #000000;
```

That would work if the graphic was specified in the HTML document.

Example:

```
<img src: "http://domain.com/background.jpg">
```

But if it is specified as a CSS background, it wouldn't show.

Example:

```
background-image: url( http://domain.com/background.jpg );
```

You can try to get the image in there like this way:

```
Code:

<table>
<!-- table stuff here -->
</table>
<img src: "http://domain.com/background.jpg"
    style: "position: relative; top: -100px; left: -10px;
z-order: -1">
```

You may have to fiddle with the top and left CSS attributes to get it where you want it, but this will make the image appear behind the table. As it's an image and not a background image, it will be printed.

Question 44: Trouble with CSS for Print

I have a form that I've used in the past to have visitors send letters via eFax to elected officials. I am trying to adapt it to enable users to print the letter in a neat looking format. Users can enter their contact information and have the option to edit a text area. Then, using a print style sheet, I formatted that information into the letter they can print off.

URL: http://www.trafficrelief.org/test.html

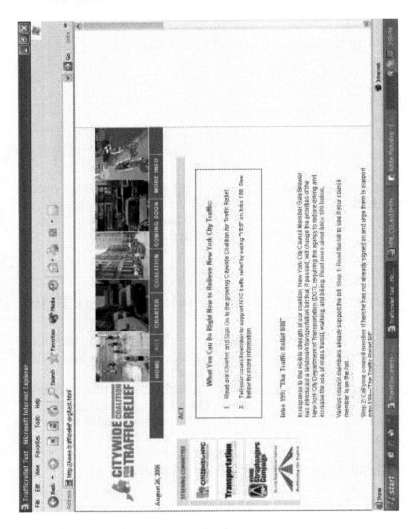

The following is my print style sheet:

```
Code:

.exclude {display:none;}

label {display: none;}

input, textarea, .print{
    border:0;
```

```
    font: normal 11pt "Times New Roman", Arial, sans-
serif;}

textarea {
    border:0;
    font: normal 11pt "Times New Roman", Arial, sans-serif;
    overflow:visible;
    width:6.70in;
    height:100%;}

#E-mail input {display:none;}

#contact {line-height:1em;
    position:absolute;
    top:50px;}

#City {width:50px;
    overflow:visible;}

#State {width:5px;
    overflow:visible;}

#subject {font-weight:bold;}

#letter {position:absolute;
    top:50px;}

#Submitted_by {position:absolute;
    top:800px;}
```

I have the beginnings of a nice letter for print but I encountered two major snags:

1. Firefox on both Mac and PC refuses to show the entire text area and mashes together the address information the user enters.

2. Safari is all over the map. It shows input borders and the text size is different. I guess its back to the drawing board for that one.

How can I solve my Firefox problems?

A: You can try to remove the 100% height from the text area declaration.

Safari has very limited styling options for form elements. This is something you'll just need to live with.

You can check this URL for more details:

http://www.456bereastreet.com/archive/200410/styling_even_more_form_controls/

You can also try to work it out by specifying a large height for the text area in inches.

Code:

```
textarea {
    border:0;
    font: normal 11pt "Times New Roman", Arial, sans-serif;
    overflow:visible;
    width:6.70in;
    height:8.5in;}
```

Menu Issues

Question 45: Tailoring CSS Image Rollover Menu in UL

I am using a CSS image rollover in conjunction with a UL in here:

http://www.newbondstreetpawnbrokers.com/new/

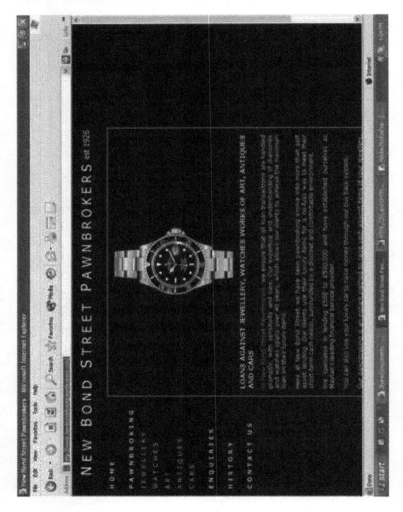

Originally, I got the CSS from here:

http://www.simplebits.com/notebook/2003/09/30/acces
sible_imagetab_rollovers.html
However, I've had to hack it to work in a vertical menu. As you can see, it's not quite right. For some reason, there is a margin to the left of the button which I don't want. It's cutting off the button so you cannot see the right hand edge of the image.

How can I make this right?

A: Your problem has to do with the default padding and/or margin applied to the UL element. If you look at the UL element by default, the text is moved inside a little bit. This is achieved either by padding, or margin, or combination of both in various browsers. In your code, your UL is kept at the default styling of the browser so that gap exists and plays a part in your button which is not showing up correctly. In your CSS, make sure you define 0 padding and margin to the UL element. It's best if it's like this:

Code:

```
#nav ul {
  padding: 0;
  margin: 0;
}
```

Question 46: CSS Dropdown Menus

I'm having a hard time getting this dropdown to align properly, and also have the "a:hover" JavaScript work in IE.

How do I make this work?

A: Check if all the CSS you have on that page is really necessary. There might be some code for a bunch of dropdowns, but might hardly be any that is actually applied. This could be causing the problems.

You can purge the CSS file a bit, and then see if you still have a problem. Also, try to give the <ul> element in your dropdown submenu a padding 0, or whatever you want. Different default padding and margins can cause this kind of problem.

Question 47: Flash Takes Focus over CSS Dropdown Menu

Flash and CSS are relatively new to me. I have an entry page with a CSS dropdown menu at the top and a flash splash below it. When a visitor hovers over the CSS menu items, some have additional items in the dropdowns. On the flash splash screen, the items in the dropdown are hiding behind the flash object.

Is there a way to make the CSS dropdown menu take focus over the flash object?

A: It is a problem with the z-index. The flash element is given a higher z-index than the other elements. Because it works like an applet, it is not an HTML element. It is a replaced element from somewhere else.

Here's one blog telling you a possible way to solve it:

http://joshuaink.com/blog/82/flash-content-and-z-index

To quote:

"...Okay, so using Drew's Flash Satay method my code for the Flash content looks something like this:

```
<object
type: "application/x-shockwave-flash" data:
"/flash/navbar.swf"
width: "750" height: "90">
<param name: "movie" value: "/flash/navbar.swf" />
<param name: "wmode" value: "transparent">
</object>"
```

Question 48: The Menu Doesn't Fit

I have managed to get the menu horizontal and even with the image for the background, but I cannot get the menu to start on the left hand side.

There is a space I cannot get rid off, and so the last menu tab is dropping to the next line.

CSS

```
Code:

/** Dropdowns **/
#nav ul { /* all lists */
padding: 0px;
margin: 0px;
list-style: none;
float: left;
width: 90px;
```

```
position:relative;
overflow:visible;

}

#nav li { /* all list items */
position: relative;
float: left;
width: 90px;
display:block;
height:auto;

}

#nav li ul { /* second-level lists */
position: absolute;
left: -1000px;
margin-left: -35px;
margin-top: 0px;
}

#nav li a {
width: 90px;
display: block;
/*font-weight: bold;*/
text-decoration: none;
padding: 0px 0px;
margin: 0;
color: #FFFFFF;
background: #5D7AC5;
text-shadow: 0px 1px 1px rgb(250,250,250);
}
#nav li a:hover {
color: #FFFFFF;
background: #5D7AC5;
border: 1px solid rgb(100,100,100);
text-shadow: 0px 0px 3px rgb(250,250,250);
}
#nav li a {
border-top: 1px solid rgb(240,240,240);
border-right: 1px solid rgb(160,160,160);
border-bottom: 1px solid rgb(160,160,160);
border-left: 1px solid rgb(240,240,240);
}

#nav a.encl {
background: #5D7AC5 center no-repeat
url('http://www.stepnstomp.co.uk/images/buttons/button1up.g
if');
border-top: 0px solid rgb(240,240,240);
border-right: 0px solid rgb(160,160,160);
border-bottom: 01px solid rgb(160,160,160);
border-left: 0px solid rgb(240,240,240);
height:25px;
```

```
padding:1px;
}

#nav a.encl:hover {
background: #5D7AC5  center no-repeat
url('http://www.stepnstomp.co.uk/images/buttons/button1up.g
if');
border-top: 0px solid rgb(240,240,240);
border-right: 0px solid rgb(160,160,160);
border-bottom: 01px solid rgb(160,160,160);
border-left: 0px solid rgb(240,240,240);
height:25px;
padding:1px;
}
#nav li:hover ul ul, #nav li:hover ul ul ul, #nav li:hover
ul ul ul ul, #nav li.iehover ul ul, #nav li.iehover ul ul
ul, #nav li.iehover ul ul ul ul {
left: -1000px;
}
#nav li:hover ul, #nav li li:hover ul, #nav li li li:hover
ul, #nav li li li li:hover ul, #nav li.iehover ul, #nav li
li.iehover ul, #nav li li li.iehover ul, #nav li li li
li.iehover ul{ /* lists nested under hovered list items */
left: auto;
}

/** Support for the "iehover-fix.js" **/
#nav iframe {
position: absolute;
left: 0;
top: 0;
z-index: 0;
filter: progid:DXImageTransform.Microsoft.Alpha(style:
0,opacity: 0);
}


/** end **/
```

Why is CSS so difficult to understand and use?

A: Most of your CSS talks about an unordered list element (<ul>) inside an element that has an id of "nav." Looking at your HTML however, the element with the id of nav is actually the UL itself. That means that some of your CSS won't be applied, or will be applied to wrong things.

I suggest that you do one of the following:

1. Change your CSS to read "ul#nav" instead of "#nav ul" in all the occurrences.

2. Give the TD that embraces the UL an id of nav and remove this id from the UL element.

It will be your choice.

You can also consider the padding left (40px) or margin left (40px) on the UL element, depending on the browser you use. The CSS you have should have fixed that gap by nullifying margins and padding on the UL element within the "#nav" element.

However, since your top UL element is not within "#nav" element, but is actually the "#nav" element itself, the padding and margins are never nullified for that element. And so, that gap appears. It's pretty straightforward and to the point, it's exactly as it should behave.

You also stated that you solved the problem and posted pictures of a horizontal menu and then you claim your menu is vertical. First you want help with getting rid of the margin/padding on the left and then you claim solution to remove the gap that does not help the menu to stack up horizontally. CSS is pretty straightforward and things behave exactly like you tell them to, you just need to use, understand and apply it correctly.

It is set in the default properties of the browser. Check where the shape of the bullet is set, where the margins for the paragraphs are set, where the borders for input elements are, and where the font size for h1 is set. All these settings have to exist and they are set by the browser's default behavior. One can very simply find the file with all these settings defined, but for IE it is more complicated and I don't know where it has them. But you do know that every element you put on your site behaves differently, so that behavior has to be defined somewhere.

Some browsers apply different initial values to others. I've found a useful practice is to "zero" everything right at the start of the style sheet. This puts all browsers on an even playing field.

At the start of your style sheet, you can put:

Code:

```
* { padding:0; margin:0; }
```

That's saying, "set the padding and margin of everything to 0."

Then it doesn't matter if IE puts 30px on something, and FF puts 35px on the same element. Now they all put a big fat nothing on there.

You can then manually set the padding and margins of your stuff as you want, and not leave it up to the browser to decide.

Question 49: .CSS/JavaScript Based Tab Menu

I am building a .CSS based menu based on two tutorials I have found.

The first is:

http://www.alistapart.com/articles/slidingdoors/

I referenced it for building the tab's graphics. But this tutorial didn't delve into the JavaScript/DHTML aspect of the navigation.

For this, I referred to:

http://www.dynamicdrive.com/dynamicindex1/ddtabmen u.htm

Using these two as a guide, I built the following:

http://www.studiocb.net/test/tab_tester2.html

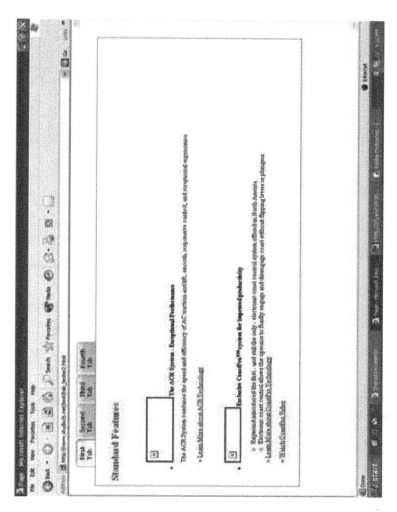

It's almost exactly what I need, except for one thing. On the currently selected tab, the right side of the "sliding door" bg image is changing per the .CSS.

Code:

```
#tablist li a.current{
background-image:url("right_on.gif");
margin-bottom:1px;
}
```

However, I need the left side bg image to change as well, but the code I have doesn't do the trick.

Code:

```
#tablist li.current{
/* background: #f7f7f7; */
background-image:url("left_on.gif");
margin-bottom:1px;
}
```

What am I missing here?

A: You're missing the fact that your left side changes when you apply ".current class" to your <li> element and you only apply that class to the <a> element.

To turn that on, you simply need to add:

```
aobject.parentNode.className :   "current"
```

At the end of your highlighttab function. However, you will still need to turn this current off for the rest of the elements. You could do the same, but I don't know how smart that is. That would require changing your function to look like this altogether:

Code:

```
function highlighttab (aobject)
{
  if (typeof tabobjlinks: : "undefined")
    collecttablinks()
  for (i: 0; i<tabobjlinks.length; i++)
  {
    tabobjlinks[i].className: ""
    tabobjlinks[i].parentNode.className: ""
  }
  aobject.className: "current"
  aobject.parentNode.className :   "current"
}
```

Question 50: Odd div Placement Issues

I'm trying to implement some CSS dropdown menus with a little JavaScript tossed in to make it work in IE.

Everything's more or less working, but I'm having some issues between browsers.

In IE it all appears fine. In Firefox, the div after the menus is placed to the far right on the screen, rather than below. If I put 3 or more brs in, then it gets put in the right place horizontally. But in IE, it shifted too far vertically and then (also you can notice the far right option Support/Contact doesn't quite highlight properly) in Opera the divs overlap, causing much of the navigation to be unusable.

You can see what I'm talking about at:

http://oculardata.com/staging

 Firefox version:

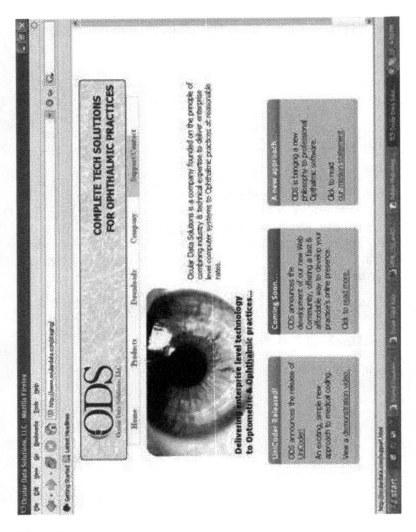

The colors, etc. are temporary.

How can I fix this problem?

A: Putting "clear: both;" on the "#mainbody" should fix the problem. I would still do away with the tables though.

Question 51: Artifacts Being Left on Screen with CSS Popup

I'm using the "pure CSS popup" from:

http://meyerweb.com/eric/css/edge/popups/demo.html

It creates a popup box on a hover action, but uses only CSS and no JavaScript. I've fixed the bugs in it so it does actually work.

The CSS code I have is:

```
div a:hover {text-decoration: none;
    border: none;}

div a span {display: none;
    padding: 5px;
    color: #000000;
    font-size: 12px;
    width: 200px;}

div a:hover span {display: block;
    position: absolute;
    top: 200px;
    left: 150px;
    width: 300px;
    padding: 5px;
    z-index: 100;
    color: black;
    border: red 2px solid;
    background: white;}
```

The HTML for it is:

```
<div id: "popup"><a href: "#">Text to MouseOver<span>Text
to pop up</span></a></div>
```

So far, the code works. But the problem is that it leaves artifacts and part of the box that pops up stays visible after leaving the text that's being hovered over, and if you mouse over the section where the box popped up, it comes up again.

I've tried playing with the positioning and it seems to only be leaving the artifacts when "position: absolute." But I've seen several other samples that use the same thing and don't leave artifacts or pop up again if you mouse over the area.

What's wrong with this and how do I fix it?

A: There is an easy solution. Add a proper doctype to your page:

```
<!DOCTYPE html PUBLIC "-//W3C//DTD HTML 4.01
Transitional//EN"
    "http://www.w3.org/TR/html4/loose.dtd">
```

Or select one from here:

_http://www.w3.org/QA/2002/04/valid-dtd-list.html

Technical Issues

Question 52: Glow/drop Shadow

Is there any way to do a text glow?

A: It's almost impossible to do effectively across-browsers. Not without using images. You can use a filter, but I'm pretty sure that's for IE only.

Other than doubling up your text layers and floating one on top of the other, your only option is to use CSS filters in IE only. Check this link below:

http://www.fred.net/dhark/demos/css/css_filter_exampl es.html

Firefox has a whole load of filters and effects, including an outline one, which might do what you want.

See the link below for a list. I don't know how complete it is, so you might want to do some searching around.

http://developer.mozilla.org/en/docs/CSS_Reference:Moz illa_Extensions

Question 53: CSS Align Issue in IE, but Works Fine in FF

I am currently creating a site but having problems aligning my CSS horizontal menu in IE.

The development link is:

http://www.bellinghamgolfclub.com/

If viewed in FF, it aligns fine with the main body. But when viewed in IE, it has an offset of about 20+px to the right.

The CSS file is:

```
#navholder {
        /*height:3.1em; */
        height: 34px;
        text-align:center;
        background:url(navbg.jpg);
        font-family:"Trebuchet MS", Verdana, Arial,
Helvetica, sans-serif;
        margin-left: auto;
        margin-right: auto;
        padding:0;
        font-size:90%;
}
ul#nav {
        margin: 0 auto;
        padding: 0;
        list-style: none;
        width:760px;
        position:relative;
        z-index:999;
}
ul.navi li {
        position: relative;
        float: left;
        list-style: none;
        width:92px;
}

ul.navi li#eventsandvenuehire {
        position: relative;
        float: left;
        list-style: none;
        width:156px;
}
```

```
li ul {
        position: absolute;
        left: 0;
        top: auto;
        display: none;
        margin:0;
        padding:0;
}

/* Styles for Menu Items */
ul li a {
        display:block;
        text-decoration:none;
        color:#fff;
        font-weight:bold;
        background:transparent; /* IE6 Bug */
        padding:0;
        border-bottom:1px solid #0E8811;
        border-right:1px solid #06aa09;       /*This is the
right border of menus*/
        height: 33px;
        line-height: 33px;
}
/* commented backslash mac hiding hack \*/
* html ul li a {height:1%}
/* end hack */

/* this sets all hovered lists background color - top
buttons*/
li:hover a, li.over a,
li:hover li a:hover, li.over li a:hover {
    color: #ffe600;
    background-color:#005103;


}
/* set dropdown to default */
li:hover li a, li.over li a {
        background:#057409;
        color:#fff;
        font-weight:normal;
        padding:0 0 0 6px;
        margin:0;
        text-align:left;
        width:145px;
        height:2em;
        line-height:2em;
}

/* Sub Menu Styles */

li:hover ul, li.over ul { display: block; }   /*The magic */

ul#nav li#homeicon { width:48px;}
```

```
ul#nav li#homeicon a {
        border-left: 1px solid #06aa09;
        background:url(/images/icon-home.gif) no-repeat 50%
50%;
        text-indent:-99em;
        margin:0;
        padding:0;
        height:33px;
}

ul#nav li#homeicon a:hover { background:url(/images/icon-
home.gif) no-repeat 50% 50% #005103; }
```

What can I do to resolve this within IE?

A: You can try the following solutions:

1. If you have an XML definition above the doctype it will throw IE into quirks mode. If you don't need it, get rid of it.

2. The way to center something in CSS is to use margins left and right as auto, and a specified width for the element you want centered. I am surprised your code works in FF.

3. When having a font name with multiple words (e.g., Trebuchet MS), put it in quotes.

4. Check to see why your banner is inside a table and why you're using tables in the first place.

Question 54: Limit the Size of an Image

```
<img src: "www.....gif">
```

How can I limit the width and height of the image?

I don't mind to cut it or put it in a box with scroll bars, but I don't want to use:

```
<img src: "www.....gif" width: "...">
```

Is there a solution for this?

A: Since CSS cropping (http://www.w3.org/TR/css3-content/#replacedContent) is not widely supported yet in the modern browsers, the only thing you could do is put it in a div that has a limited width and height and put "overflow: auto;" on the div to make it scroll (or "overflow: hidden;" if you want to just cut it).

Question 55: CSS Image Swap

I am running a CSS menu system with the following code:

```
/*----- MENU CSS
-----------------------------------*/
#nav, #nav ul { /* all lists */
  padding: 0;
  margin: 0;
  list-style: none;
  float : left;
  width : 11em;
  border :0;
}
#nav li { /* all list items */
background:url("http://www.blogblog.com/rounders3/icon_arro
w_sm.gif") no-repeat 2px .25em;
  position : relative;
  float : left;
  line-height : 1.25em;
  margin-bottom : 0;
  width: 11em;
  border :0;
}
#nav li ul { /* second-level lists */
 position : absolute;
 left: -999em;
 margin-left : -13.3em;
 margin-top : -1em;
 border-bottom:0px dotted #345;
 line-height:1.4em;
 background:#234;
}
#nav li ul ul { /* third-and-above-level lists */
  left: -999em;
  margin-left : -13.3em;
  margin-top : -1em;
  background:#234;
}
#nav li a {
  width: 11em;
  display : block;
  color : #CCCC99;
  text-decoration : none;
  background:#234;
  padding : 0 0.5em;
}
#nav li a:hover {
  color : #00FFFF;
  background:#234
```

```
}
#nav li:hover ul ul, #nav li:hover ul ul ul, #nav
li.sfhover ul ul, #nav li.sfhover ul ul ul {
  left: -999em;
}
#nav li:hover ul, #nav li li:hover ul, #nav li li li:hover
ul, #nav li.sfhover ul, #nav li li.sfhover ul, #nav li li
li.sfhover ul {
  left: auto;
}
```

The menu behaves well. What I would like to accomplish is a simple image reversal on mouse-over. When I change the "#nav li a:hover" part of the code is as follows:

from:

```
#nav li a:hover {
  color : #00FFFF;
  background:#234
```

to:

```
#nav li a:hover {
  color : #00FFFF;
  background:url("http://www.abc.com/myimages/i
mageA.jpg") no-repeat 2px .25em;
```

I can see the image on mouse over, but the image is staying just to the right of the original image. I'm not having any luck making it appear as a swapping of images.

You can see this effect on this page (look under "Primary References" for the effect, just mouse over a menu item). The hover image appears but just off to the right of the original.

Do you have any ideas on how to fix this?

A: Your original background image is on the <li> element, while the changed one is on the <a> element. So, you will never get them to align, since anchor does not even exist where the background image of the <li> element is. All you need to do is apply the background to the "li" element instead of the anchor one:

```
#nav li:hover,
#nav li.sfhover {
  background:url("image.jpg") no-repeat 2px .25em;
}
```

That being said and taking into consideration that your image is pretty small. It is still a better idea to perform the background change as described here:

http://wellstyled.com/css-nopreload-rollovers.html

Question 56: Convert Tables to CSS Div/Span

I have a web page with the main data, but for aesthetics I want 2 bars up and down either side of the main page.

In tables, I would do it like this:

```
<table>
  <tr>
    <td height: "100%"> imageleft.jpg </td>
    <td> main page with lots of asp coding and div blocks
further down the page</td>
    <td height: "100%"> imageright.jpg </td>
  </tr>
</table
```

This is working fine at the moment and I have div tags for some ASP scripting later in the page. Also, the color of the main page is white but the edge tables would be a light grey. The problem is, as soon as I go to print the page it cuts off when the first div tag starts but I want to print the entire page.

Is it easier to convert that table from the above to div or span tags (how ever that is done), or is there some other printing thing I'm not aware of?

It's is just a simple pixel image, basically a border from a pre-design stage.

The left image is 1px wide, but the right image is 2px wide so there's no border detail.

In design I usually use the table idea with bigger variations of this, so it still looks good.

How can I fix this?

A: First, you're talking about two strips running down each side of your main content container. This is easy to do, say like this:

Code:

```
<style type: "text/css">
#mainContainer {
  border-left: 1px solid blue;
  border-right: 2px solid blue;
}
```

This would create something like what you described.

However, if you're looking at a three column approach, I suggest you go with floats.

To tell you the truth, printing floated elements is a pain as it is badly implemented in the browsers. However, think about the printing. CSS allows you to specify a printing style sheet that is only visible when printing (or print previewing) the document and not on the screen itself. In there, you can remove all the non-necessary elements and style your main column to be 100% wide. If not, I suggest you reprogram the columns so that the content prints first and the floated left and right columns print after that.

Question 57: Tool to Show what CSS is Applied to HTML Element

I'm trying to unravel a CSS style sheet to determine what CSS is applied to a particular HTML element. It's taking a lot of time to figure out the precedence of CSS styles and many elements in the HTML have multiple classes assigned to them on top of the styles applied to all HTML tags.

Do you know of a tool that can show me exactly what CSS styles are being applied to a particular HTML element?

A: FireFox has a 'Tool' called the "DOM Inspector" that works great.

You might also download the Web Developer Toolbar Extension for Firefox.

Under the CSS menu, you can choose "View Style Information." Clicking on a page element will then open a window showing the styles for that element.

Question 58: Changing Text Color

I've tweaked a submit button on my page with a bit of CSS. But is it possible to have the text color in it changes when hovering over it, ideally with an inline style?

Code:

```
<input type: "submit" name: "submit" style: "background-
color:#003360; font-size:10pt; color:white; font-
family:Arial; font-weight:bold; font-style:italic;
cursor:pointer; width:120; border:none" value: "+ Add an
account" onClick: "document.warrantEdit.action:
'process.asp?Action: AddAccount';">
```

A: You could create a class for the submit button and put your styles in there.

Then, use the ":hover" pseudo class to change the style when it's hovered over. However, IE is probably not going to work unless you also whack in some JavaScript, so you may as well use JavaScript to do the style change.

I would advise taking out the inline style and creating a class or ID rule though. Also bear in mind that IE only supports the ":hover" pseudo class on <a> elements.

A right pain, but it can normally be taken around with a small piece of JavaScript (at least until IE supports ":hover").

Here's an example that's pretty easy to implement:

```
<style type: "text/css">

input.out {
    border:1px solid purple;
    color:purple;
    background-color:yellow;
}

input.over {
```

```
    border:1px solid yellow;
    color:yellow;
    background-color:purple;
}

</style>
<script type: "text/javascript">

function over(obj, bool) {
    obj.className :  (bool) ? "over" : "out";
}

</script>
<input type: "button" value: "hover over me" onmouseover:
"over(this, true)" onmouseout: "over(this, false)" class:
"out" />
```

Question 59: Containing Text in One Scrollable Area

I'm designing a website which has fixed dimensions. Consequently, I would like to have an area of text that fits within these fixed dimensions and is scrollable when the body of text is too large to be fully contained in the text area. I've seen it in the past on a number of sites, but can't find any right now.

Is it a big no-no in terms of usability? If not, how would I go about achieving this? Is it something that all browsers can support?

A: Depending on the object you are using (div, p, td, etc.), you should be able to set static heights and widths using a style definition, along with utilizing the overflow style definition; set overflow to auto or scroll. This will enable scrolling for all content that exceeds the dimensions of your object, while keeping the size intact.

```
Code:

<div style: "width: 100px; height: 100px; overflow: auto;">
  Lotsa content here.
</div>
```

This div box will be 100px wide and 100px high and if there is a lot of text inside, scrollbars will appear. It is not a big no-no in design if there is a specific use for it. Say, if you want to put all your content in such a box and use a special scrollbar for it, I would advise against it because most users would expect a scrollbar at far right or left, depending on their browser orientation. If it is a small box containing latest news, updates, shout box or something like that, giving it scrollbars where there's more content is perfectly acceptable.

All modern browsers that support CSS will support this.

In a final version, move the CSS style to a separate style sheet. Think if <div> is the best element. Depending on the content, you might just want to use a paragraph (if it is only a text) or a list element (if it is a list).

You have to know how big will your fixed section be in how it will behave in different screen resolutions. You can assume that hardly anyone is using 640x480 nowadays.

However, someone with 1024, a sidebar and a browser window that is not maximized might have a viewing area of 640px wide. If such, a user gets the main scrollbar to scroll around your design and inner scrollbar to scroll around your content, they're lost as a user. That's something worth considering I believe.

Question 60: Link Colors

I cant decide which colors would my links be using, the "body" tag, "link," "alink," and "vlink" attributes.

What if I want each link to have different colors? Is it possible to do in HTML?

A: If you are using CSS it is. I'd advise not using the body attributes, favoring CSS for all links:

Code:

```
<!DOCTYPE html PUBLIC "-//W3C//DTD HTML 4.01//EN"
"http://www.w3.org/TR/html4/strict.dtd">
<html lang: "en">
<head>
    <meta http-equiv: "content-type" content: "text/html;
charset: iso-8859-1">
    <meta http-equiv: "content-language" content: "en">
    <title>Link colour demo</title>

    <style type: "text/css">
        /* Style all links a default colour */
        a, a:link            { color: #0000FF; }
        a:visited            { color: #FF00FF; }
        a:hover              { color: #FF0000; }
        a:active, a:focus    { color: #00FF00; }

        /* Override some other link behavior */
        .redLinksContainer a, .redLinksContainer
a:link        { color: #FF0000; }
        a.blueLink,
a.blueLink:link                          { color:
#0000FF; }
        a.greenLink,
a.greenLink:link                         { color: #00FF00; }
    </style>
</head>

<body>
    <div>
        <a href: "http://www.google.co.uk/">Go to
Google</a><br />
        <a href: "http://www.yahoo.co.uk/">Go to Yahoo!</a>
    <div>
    <div class: "redLinksContainer">
        <a href: "http://www.google.co.uk/">Go to
```

```
Google</a><br />
        <a href: "http://www.yahoo.co.uk/">Go to Yahoo!</a>
    </div>
    <div>
        <a class: "blueLink" href:
"http://www.google.co.uk/">Go to Google</a><br />
        <a class: "greenLink" href:
"http://www.yahoo.co.uk/">Go to Yahoo!</a>
    </div>
</body>
</html>
```

That's not a perfect example, as I've not tried to override
certain pseudo-classes for some links, but you get the idea.

Question 61: News Boxes

I've just been looking at the MSN site and noticed the
boxes they have had section off their content.

Unfortunately, the source code for the site is a nightmare
to pick apart. What's the best way to achieve this in CSS?

A: You can create a DIV with an H2 in it and style them
both to look similar.

Question 62: Select Box CSS

I'm trying to apply a CSS to a drop down box. As you can see, I stuck the " class: "dropdown" " in there but that didn't worked.

I also tried to call it just by using the id select in my CSS file. What am I doing wrong?

Code:

```
<select name: "selectName" size: "1" class: "dropdown">
<option value: "one">first</option>
<option value: "two">second</option>
<option value: "three">third</option>
</select>
```

A: You can use the class like that with no problem.

"<select> items" are part of the user's OS rather than the browser and as such there is little you can do to style/control them.

Question 63: CSS Fluid Layout with PHP Inclusion

I've been trying to create a pure CSS fluid layout with this tutorial:

http://www.tjkdesign.com/articles/liquid/7.asp

However, I wanted to make the layout with PHP inclusion. If I update something for example the menu, I would only have to edit one page.

The layout works fine in Mozilla Firefox. However, in Internet Explorer it does not. Here are some of the main problems:

1. Layout spans the entire width of the page.
2. The dark background image is nowhere to be seen.
3. The layout is not centered as it's supposed to be.

I have tried some things that would make the layout sort of work, including putting a large div around the other divs, or using fixed widths instead of fluid. However, I am trying to make the layout as simple as possible, so I'm trying to avoid using such tactics.

Does it have something to do with my coding?

Here are the links to pages you would probably want to take a look at:

The CSS:

http://www.kaidan.org/testing2/style2.css

The Index Page:

http://www.kaidan.org/testing2/index.php

A: You should include a doctype on your page. This will make or sometimes break much of your design.

You can pick from of this site:

http://www.w3.org/QA/2002/04/valid-dtd-list.html

Question 64: Position of Form Submit Button

I want to position two buttons for my form. I would like a little space between, and for them to be centered on the form. I have the "text-align: center;" on the form, but the buttons do not seem to follow.

How can I do it right?

A: This should work:

Code:

```
<div style: "text-align:center;">
    <input type: "button" ... style: "margin-right: 10px;">
    <input type: "button" ... >
</div>
```

If it doesn't work, check to see if you have some other styling in your CSS that is causing problems.

You can also check if it is the "float: left" and "display: block" applied to all inputs that is causing the problem. Remove this from generic inputs and apply it using a class, then you'll be sorted.

Question 65: CSS Positioning

I'm making my first attempt at using CSS to position things rather than just set fonts and stuff. I've been trying to learn it on my own with online documentss I find but it's getting confusing. What I'm trying to do is take chord symbols and lyrics from a database of songs and lay them out such that each chord lines up above its associated word. My first attempt to use a code looks like this:

Code:

```
<style>.lyrics { font-size: 12pt; margin-bottom: 0; margin-
top: 14pt; font-family: Arial, Helvetica;}
.chord { position:relative; left:0px; top:-14pt; font-size:
12pt; color:red; font-weight:bold; font-family: Arial,
Helvetica; }
</style></head>
<body><p class: lyrics><span class: chord>D</span>Great in
power, <span class: chord>Bm</span>great in glory</p>
<p class: lyrics><span class: chord>G</span>Great in mercy,
<span class: chord>Em</span>King of <span class:
chord>A</span>heaven</p>
<p class: lyrics><span class: chord>D</span>Great in
battle, <span class: chord>Bm</span>great in wonder</p>
<p class: lyrics><span class: chord>G</span>Great in Zion,
<span class: chord>Em</span>King over <span class:
chord>Asus A</span>all the <span class:
chord>D</span>earth</p>
```

But the horizontal space for each chord is still there between the words. I want the words to have their normal spacing and the chord's left edge to be lined up with whatever the next character is (after the span, the way I have it now).

How can I do that? I assume it has to do with span vs. div, or position types, or something.

A: Try this:

Code:

```
<html>
<head>
    <style type: "text/css">
        .lyrics { position: relative; font-size: 12pt;
margin-bottom: 0; margin-top: 14pt; font-family: Arial,
Helvetica;}
        .chord { position:absolute; top:-14pt; font-size:
12pt; color:red; font-weight:bold; font-family: Arial,
Helvetica; }
    </style>
</head>

<body>
    <p class: lyrics><span class: chord>D</span>Great in
power, <span class: chord>Bm</span>great in glory</p>
    <p class: lyrics><span class: chord>G</span>Great in
mercy, <span class: chord>Em</span>King of <span class:
chord>A</span>heaven</p>
    <p class: lyrics><span class: chord>D</span>Great in
battle, <span class: chord>Bm</span>great in wonder</p>
    <p class: lyrics><span class: chord>G</span>Great in
Zion, <span class: chord>Em</span>King over <span class:
chord>Asus A</span>all the <span class:
chord>D</span>earth</p>
</body>
</html>
```

I've added a type to your style declaration. You should
always have one of these. I've also added the missing html,
head, body tags (some open or closing tags were missing
altogether).

In the CSS, I added a "position: relative" to the lyrics
paragraph so that the chords would be positioned relative
to them and removed the left positioning from the chords,
so they stayed at their default position.

The last change was to make the chords absolutely
positioned which removed them from the document flow
and thus removed the space they took up.

For additional information on placing "heading" element -
<h1>, <h2>, whatever, blank lines between stanzas/verses
can be handled with margins. You just need some kind of
block element, it's something like this:

Code:

```
<h1>Great in Power</h1>
<div class: "verse">
   <p><span>D</span>Great in power, <span>Bm</span>great in
glory</p>
   <p><span>G</span>Great in mercy, <span>Em</span>King of
<span>A</span>heaven</p>
</div>
<div class: "verse">
   <p><span>D</span>Great in battle, <span>Bm</span>great in
wonder</p>
   <p><span>G</span>Great in Zion, <span>Em</span>King over
<span>Asus A</span>all the <span>D</span>earth</p>
</div>
```

I'm not that struck on <p> elements for each line either, but we'll let that pass.

Now you style it like this:

Code:

```
.verse {margin-bottom: 2em; }

.verse p { position: relative; font-size: 12pt; margin-
bottom: 0; margin-top: 14pt; font-family: Arial, Helvetica;
white-space: nowrap;}

.verse p span { position:absolute; top:-14pt; color:red;
font-weight:bold; }
```

Note how I've only used a single class and used the other elements' position below the classed element to identify them which saves a lot of typing. I've also not repeated properties like font-family in the <span> rule, that will be inherited from the <p> anyway.

Question 66: Style/link in Body Tag

I've hit a snag validating my code. I know it's my fault with the way my template/SSI design has been implemented. But changing it will require a complete re-write.

The validator doesn't like the fact that I have CSS styles linked into the page from the body tag, so it won't validate. The CSS is still linked in correctly and the page displays okay.

Is this a big problem? It's not 100% semantically correct. I'm never going to reach that because I'm not prepared to drop my tables for layout.

It's not semantically correct, but does linking in a CSS style in the body actually make the browser behave differently, it's not like missing an </>or /> end tag?

What I'm getting at is some rules that can be bent, isn't that what CSS hacks are all about?

Is placing a style in the body one of those rules that can be bent or do I honestly need to redesign my whole template system to truly validate?

If the only error in the code was having a <style> tag in the body, is that fair?

A: It's one of the rules that can't be bent. Yes, at the moment every browser is still supporting style tags inside body tags, but in the future, you don't know what will happen. And having them where they shouldn't be opens you up for possible display errors.

I really don't see what the big deal is. If you have style tags in the head or even better in a separate style sheet, it shouldn't change your output in any way.

Just put everything that has to do with the style sheet is into a separate CSS file. You can even create a multiple CSS files and link all of them.

Question 67: My Site is Different in IE and FF

I have built my site and have been testing it in FF and IE. When displayed in IE, it puts the navigation bar where I want it. But in FF, it displays it further to the right.

To get a visual, you can look at it:

http://www.mbgolfsociety.co.uk

My CSS code follows (I have left some out that aren't relevant to this query):

```
Code:

body{
    font-family:Georgia, "Times New Roman", Times, serif;
    margin:0;
}
#main_nifty {
    position: relative;
    background-color: #A0D6A4;
    width: 970px;
    height: auto;
    margin: 1em 1em 1em 1em;
    overflow:auto;
}
#container{
    background:#A0D6A4;
    float: left;
    width: 700px;
    margin-top:4em;
    margin-bottom:1em;
    margin-left:1em;
```

```
    margin-right:0.5em;
    }
#menu{
    background:#A0D6A4;
    float: left;
    height: auto;
    width: 220px;
    margin-bottom:1em;
}
#bottom{
    background:#A0D6A4;
    margin: 1em 1em 1em 1em;
    color: #A0D6A4;
    clear: both;
}
#menu ul{
    margin-left: 1em;
    margin-top:4em;
    list-style: none;
}
#menu li{
    font-size:120%;
    margin-bottom:1em;
    font-family:Georgia, "Times New Roman", Times, serif;
}
#menu img{
    float:left;
    padding:0;
}
#menu a:link, #menu a:visited{
    font-size:115%;
    color:#000000;
    font-weight:normal;
    text-decoration:none;
}
#menu a:hover{
    color:#990033;
}
```

The code for my template is:

```
<%@LANGUAGE: "VBSCRIPT" CODEPAGE: "1252"%>
<!DOCTYPE html PUBLIC "-//W3C//DTD XHTML 1.0
Transitional//EN" "http://www.w3.org/TR/xhtml1/DTD/xhtml1-
transitional.dtd">
<html xmlns: "http://www.w3.org/1999/xhtml" lang: "en"
xml:lang: "en">
<head>
<script type: "text/javascript" src:
"/includes/nifty.js"></script>
<script type: "text/javascript" src:
"/includes/layout.js"></script>
<!--#include virtual: "/includes/includes.asp"-->
```

```
<link href: "/css/menu.css" rel: "stylesheet" type:
"text/css" />
<link rel: "stylesheet" type: "text/css" href:
"/css/niftyPrint.css" media: "print" />
<!-- TemplateBeginEditable name: "doctitle" -->
<title>M&amp;B Golf Society</title>
<!-- TemplateEndEditable -->
<meta http-equiv: "Content-Type" content: "text/html;
charset: iso-8859-1" />
<!-- TemplateBeginEditable name: "head" -->
<!-- TemplateEndEditable -->
<%
' *** Logout the current user.
dim logout
logout: request.querystring("logout")
If logout: 1 then
  Session.Contents.Remove("sess_User_Logname")
 End If
%>

</head>
<body>
<!--open main_nifty which wraps around all of the menu &
container-->
<div id: "main_nifty">
    <!--open menu-->
  <div id: "menu">
    <ul>
      <li><img src: "/images/golf_ball.gif" alt:
"golf_ball" /><a href: "/navigation/home.asp">Home</a></li>
       <li><img src: "/images/golf_ball.gif" alt:
"golf_ball" /><a href:
"/navigation/fixtures.asp">Fixtures</a></li>
       <li><img src: "/images/golf_ball.gif" alt:
"golf_ball" /><a href:
"/navigation/results.asp">Results</a></li>
       <li><img src: "/images/golf_ball.gif" alt:
"golf_ball" /><a href:
"/navigation/winners.asp">Winners</a></li>
       <li><img src: "/images/golf_ball.gif" alt:
"golf_ball" /><a href:
"/navigation/handicaps.asp">Handicaps</a></li>
       <li><img src: "/images/golf_ball.gif" alt:
"golf_ball" /><a href:
"/navigation/members.asp">Membership</a></li>
       <li><img src: "/images/golf_ball.gif" alt:
"golf_ball" /><a href: "/navigation/contact.asp">Contact
        Us</a></li>
    </ul>
  </div>
  <!--close menu-->
  <!--open container this is where all of the content goes-
->
  <div id: "container"> <!-- TemplateBeginEditable name:
```

```
"main_layer" --> this is
    where you can edit </font><!-- TemplateEndEditable -->
    <!--close container-->
  </div>
  <!--open bottom this is where copyright etc goes-->
  <div id: "bottom">
    <p class: "privacy"><a class: "secret" href:
"/navigation/login.asp">Design by
    John Flood</a> | <a href: "http://www.w3.org/">Built
to W3C Standards</a>
      | <a href:
"/navigation/accessibility.asp">Accessibility</a> | <a
href: "/navigation/links.asp">Links</a></p>
    <a href: "http://validator.w3.org/check?uri:
referer"><img class: "w3c"
        src: "http://www.w3.org/Icons/valid-xhtml10"
        alt: "Valid XHTML 1.0 Transitional" height: "31"
width: "88" /></a>
    <!--close bottom-->
    <!--close main_nifty-->
  </div>
</div>
</body>
</html>
```

All the site works, but it's annoying me why it won't display properly. I've tried messing around with different widths, etc., but to no avail.

What am I missing here?

A: IE and FF use different methods to indent the lists. While IE uses margins for this, FF uses padding. Your UL (#menu UL) has specified margin-left which changes the default margin in IE to whatever you want (1em). It has no setting for padding-left, which then stays at its default value in FF (which is 40px).

So, your UL element has a padding of 40px in FF and none in IE. If you nullify the padding-left in CSS, you should get equal results.

```
Code:

#menu ul{
    margin-left: 1em;
    margin-top:4em;
```

```
    list-style: none;
    padding-left: 0;
}
```

Question 68: Dynamic CSS, Another FF Vs. IE

Why does the following code and script work fine in FF but not with IE?

Code:

```
<!DOCTYPE HTML PUBLIC "-//W3C//DTD HTML 4.01
Transitional//EN"
    "http://www.w3.org/TR/html4/loose.dtd">
<html>
<head>
<title>Test Css</title>
<style type: "text/css" media: "all" id: "mood">@import
url("main.css");</style>
<style type: "text/css">
.btn{
    border:groove gray 2px;
    background:black;
    color:white;
    text-align:center;
    cursor:pointer;
        width:100px;
    }
</style>
</head>
<body>
<div id: "btnmood">
<div id: "default" class: "btn" onclick:
'mood("main");'> Normal </div>
<br />
<div id: "dark" class: "btn" onclick:
"mood(this.id);"> Dark </div>

</div>
<script type: "text/javascript">
function mood(m){
//alert(m);
var jj: document.getElementById('mood');
jj.innerHTML: '@import url(\"' +m+ '.css\");';
    }
</script>
```

```
</body>
</html>
```

And main.css is:

```
body{
    background:orange;
}
```

```
with dark.css being:
```

```
body{
    background:darkblue;
}
```

```
The example is here:
```

http://jj4.org/test.html

```
IE Error: "unknown runtime error".
```

What can be the reason for this?

A: I'm not the expert on browser implementation of JavaScript, but a runtime error is always some script (not just HTML/CSS) and you only have two lines in your JS routine. The first is a very normal access of a DOM element, but the second one (importing a CSS file) seems pretty bold, so I would suspect that. Have you commented that out and seen whether the error goes away? Obviously you want to get it working, but the first question is simply which line is the problem.

If the problem is indeed the import and your CSS files are indeed just one line, I suggest simply specifying the body background in JS rather than trying to import a one-line file:

```
Code:
```

```
function mood(m){
var jj: document.getElementById('mood');
if (m: "main") {
  document.body.bgColor: "orange";
} else {
```

```
   document.body.bgColor: "darkblue";
}
```

If this is just a test before doing something with a lot of changes or you want to change color schemes simply by swapping out files, then I guess you'll still need the external file. Here's a routine I found to get the file in there by more standard JavaScript code (I simplified it to the relevant parts):

Code:

```
var CSSAdd;
function AddCSS(name){
 head: document.getElementsByTagName('HEAD')[0];
 // next line removes the previously added StyleSheet
 if (CSSAdd){ head.removeChild(CSSAdd); }
 CSSAdd: document.createElement('LINK');
 CSSAdd.rel: 'stylesheet';
 CSSAdd.type: 'text/css';
 CSSAdd.href: name;
 head.appendChild(CSSAdd);
}
```

In your case, you would call the function once at load time with "main.css" as the parameter (rather than linking the CSS file directly in HTML), so that the "CSSAdd" variable gets set correctly. Use and modify as needed, I simply copy/pasted it here.

Question 69: Visited Links Not Displaying Correctly

I've got two styles for links; "mostlinks" works flawlessly and "sublinks" works except for the "visited" property. For whatever reason, the "A.sublinks:visited" line isn't working, though I copied it directly from "A.mostlinks:visited" and just changed "most" to "sub." When a link has been visited, my font family and font color changes to the browser's default.

My CSS file:

```
A.mostlinks:link {text-decoration: none; color:
rgb(237,0,140); font-family: "Helvetica"; font-size:11px;
line-height: 20px;}
A.mostlinks:visited {text-decoration: none; color:
rgb(237,0,140); font-family: "Helvetica"; font-size:11px;
line-height: 20px;}
A.mostlinks:active {text-decoration: none; color:
rgb(237,0,140); font-family: "Helvetica"; font-size:11px;
line-height: 20px;}
A.mostlinks:hover {text-decoration: none; color:
rgb(75,75,75); font-family: "Helvetica"; font-size:11px;
line-height: 20px;}

A.sublinks:link {text-decoration: none; color:
rgb(75,75,75); font-family: "Helvetica"; font-size:11px;
line-height: 20px;}
A.sublinks:visited {text-decoration: none; color:
rgb(75,75,75); font-family: "Helvetica"; font-size:11px;
line-height: 20px;}
A.sublinks:active {text-decoration: none; color:
rgb(75,75,75); font-family: "Helvetica"; font-size:11px;
line-height: 20px;}
A.sublinks:hover {text-decoration: none; color:
rgb(237,0,140); font-family: "Helvetica"; font-size:11px;
line-height: 20px;}
```

The problematic link:

```
<td height: 350 width: 220 valign: top align: left><b>
<br>
<a class: sublinks href: "http://www.economist.com"
onMouseOver: "targetbox.src: 'images/economist.jpg';"
onmouseout: "targetbox.src: 'images/targetbox.jpg';"> The
Economist</a><br>
```

```
</b>
</td>
```

How can I make this right?

A: It looks like your styles were overwritten by something else. Just a few CSS pointers:

1. Order pseudo classes in correct order to get them to work correctly:

```
:link, :visited, :hover, :active
```

2. Use inheritance. All pseudo styles will follow the main style defined just for the element/class/id. Your code could be reduced to this (without any penalties):

```
Code:

A.mostlinks { text-decoration: none; color: rgb(237,0,140);
font-family: "Helvetica", sans-serif; font-size: 11px;
line-height: 20px; }
A.mostlinks:hover { color: rgb(75,75,75); }

A.sublinks { text-decoration: none; color: rgb(75,75,75);
font-family: "Helvetica", sans-serif; font-size:11px; line-
height: 20px; }
A.sublinks:hover { color: rgb(237,0,140); }
```

3. Always specify a generic font in the font-family declaration (see the code above).

4. Avoid classing each element and consider dependencies.

Question 70: Changing Link Color in a Table using CSS

I have created an HTML document with a style sheet that alters the color of an anchor <A> tag on hover (i.e., the link turns white on mouse over). This works on all my links on the page, except for the ones that are in a table.

How can I fix this?

A: You can insert this code into your style sheet:

Code:

```
TD A:hover {color: white;}
```

HTML and CSS Combo

Question 71: Negative Values for Margins

I have a top and bottom margin on both the h2 and p elements set to 0 in my style sheet and that still did not get the paragraph close enough to the heading. I gave it a negative value and got it right up under the heading as I wanted. I couldn't find out whether this was non-standard or not.

Is there a better way to do it?

Also, instead of the <br> tags for my listings of my universities and certifications, is there a more standard way?

Code:

```
<!DOCTYPE HTML PUBLIC "-//W3C//DTD HTML 4.01//EN"
"http://www.w3.org/TR/html4/strict.dtd">

<html>

<head>
    <title>Owen Peery: Education</title>
        <meta http-equiv: "content-type" content:
"text/html; charset: iso-8859-1">
        <meta name: "generator" content: "HAPedit 3.1">


<link rel: "stylesheet" type: "text/css" href:
"niftyCorners.css">
<link rel: "stylesheet" type: "text/css" href:
"niftyPrint.css" media: "print">
<link rel: "stylesheet" type: "text/css" href:
"resumestyle.css">

<script type: "text/javascript" src: "nifty.js"></script>
<script type: "text/javascript">
window.onload: function(){
if(!NiftyCheck())
    return;
Rounded("div#content","all","#B0BFC2","#BBDB88","smooth");
Rounded("div#nav","tl bl","#B0BFC2","#FACD8A","smooth");
}
</script>
```

```
</head>

<body>
    <div id: "container">
        <div id: "nav">

                <ul>
                    <li><a href: "index.html">Home</a></li>
                    <li><a href:
"education.html">Education</a></li>
                    <li><a href: "workexperience.html">Work
Experience</a></li>
                    <li><a href:
"relatedexperience.html">Related Experience</a></li>
                    <li><a href:
"technologyskills.html">Technology Skills</a></li>
                </ul>

        </div>
        <div id: "content">
                <h1>Owen Peery
                </h1>


                <h2>
                    Education
                </h2>
                <p>
                    University of California at
Berkeley<br>
                    BA in History, minor in City
Planning<br>
                    graduated 1993
                </p>

                <p>
                    Holy Names College<br>
                    CA teaching credential, MA in Urban
Education, ABT<br>
                    Thesis currently being researched<br>
                    attended 1998-2002
                </p>

                <p>
                    University of the Arts<br>
                    Continuing Education<br>
                    Design courses: Photoshop and Web
Design levels 1 and 2,<br>
                    attended 2004-2006
                </p>

                <p>
                    PTEC - Continuing Education and
Professional Development<br>
```

```
                    Intro and Intermediate level courses:
Word, Excel, and Powerpoint<br>
                    Intro to iPhoto and iTunes<br>
                    Netrekker<br>
                    Schoolnet
              </p>

              <h2>
                    Certifications
              </h2>
              <p>
                    PA Elementary Education, 2005<br>
                    PA Business, Computers, Information
Technology, 2005<br>
                    PA Master's Equivalency, 2005<br>
                    CA Elementary Education, 2002<br>
                    CA Supplemental Authorization for
Social Studies, 2002<br>
              </p>

      </div>
</div>

</body>

</html>
```

CSS:

```
              body
              {
              padding: 20px;
              background-color: #B0BFC2;
              text-align: center;
              font: 95% Verdana,Arial,sans-serif;
              }

              h1
              {
              font-size: 250%;
              color: #FFF;
              letter-spacing: 1px;
              margin: 0;
              padding: 0 0 10px 10px;
              }

              h2
              {
              font-size: 150%;
              color: #FFF;
              margin: 0;
              margin-bottom: -10px;
              padding: 0 0 10px 10px;
              }
```

```
p
{
margin: 0;
padding: 0 0 10px 10px;
}

div#container
{
width:700px;
margin: 0 left;
text-align:left;
}

div#content
{
float:right;
width:515px;
background: #BBDB88;
}

div#nav
{
float:left;
width:180px;
margin-top:40px;
background: #FACD8A;
}

#nav ul
{
margin: 10px;
padding: 0;
list-style-type: none;
text-align: right;
line-height: 250%;
}


a
{
text-decoration: none;
}

a:link
{
color: black;
}

a:visited
{
color: black;
}

a:hover
```

```
        {
        color: orange;
        }
```

Incidentally, if I use the shorthand margin statement:

```
margin: 0 -10px 0 0
```

I don't get the effect I wanted, but when I use:

```
margin: 0;
    margin-bottom: -10px;
```

I get the effect, at least in FF for now. But why is this?

Back to the <br> tags, should I use an unordered list with "text decoration none" and each line will be a list item? It is a listing of universities and certifications but a simple list won't give me the breaks where I want them.

Can I use list item tags where I want the breaks?

A: Negative margins are perfectly acceptable and if they give you the effect you were looking for (a sort of overlaying effect) then you should use it. Just make sure it looks acceptable on all browsers.

As for your second question:

Quote:
"Also instead of the <br> tags for my **listings** of my universities and certifications, is there a better way? When I say better, I mean more standards conforming."

You've answered your own question. For listings, use lists. Be it definition lists, ordered, or unordered lists, whichever fits best.

First is the margin. Shorthand property when giving four values works like this. You begin with the top and then set the others in a clockwise fashion.

Like the following:

```
Code:

margin: top right bottom left;
```

So, you're setting right margin to 10px in your first example, not the bottom one.

Second, the br tags. I am thinking maybe you could go with the definition lists. Here's a good page describing (and showing) different ways you can style those.

The link:

http://www.maxdesign.com.au/presentation/definition/

Question 72: FireFox - Menu Flashing

I've validated my CSS and my XHTML and all seems okay. However, in FireFox, when you hover over a menu item, the first menu seems to flash the content of the menu you hover over.

Why is this happening in FF and how can I fix it?

Here is the information on my FF:

```
Mozilla/5.0 (Windows; U; Windows NT 5.1; en-US; rv:1.7.12)
Gecko/20050915 Firefox/1.0.7
```

Is it a bug with the version of FF I've got, rather than my code?

A: Check what version you are using.

If I roll over the tabbed menu items (Company, Guestbook, Music, etc.), the sub-menus appear acceptable. Rolling over any of those sub-menu items highlights them with no problems. Or perhaps it's an Fx 1.0.7 glitch that was resolved.

Check if you can upgrade your FireFox, it might be a bug in the older version of FF.

Question 73: Position: relative and Line Wrapping

Here is my original and favorite way of placing chords above song lyrics. It's a piece of the style definitions followed by a piece of one song, which is inside a bordered table so it has a width limit and ends up wrapping:

Code:

```
.chordlyrics {
  font-family: Arial, Helvetica, sans-serif;
  font-size: 10pt;
  margin-top: 11pt;
  margin-bottom: 0;
  position: relative}
.chord {
  font-family: Arial, Helvetica, sans-serif;
  font-size: 10pt;
  font-weight: bold;
  color: #E00000;
  position: absolute;
  top: -10pt; }

<p class: chordlyrics><span class: chord>Em</span>You
search much <span class: chord>D/F#</span>deeper with<span
class: chord>A</span>in, through the way things ap<span
class: chord>Em</span>pear</p>
<p class: chordlyrics>You're looking <span class:
chord>D/F#</span>into my <span class:
chord>A</span>heart</p>
```

A screen capture of the results can be seen here:

http://proverbs2525.org/tektips/wrapping1.jpg

As you can see, the "Em" that should appear above the word "appear," doesn't. It stays above the first line of the paragraph, clumping illegibly with other chords.

Another way I have tried to do this is by replacing "margin-top:11pt" with "margin-top:0;line-height:21pt" to make room for the chords on the wrapped line. That result can be seen at:

http://proverbs2525.org/tektips/wrapping2.jpg

The wrapped line indeed does leave room for the chord, but there is no improvement in where the chord is written. Also, apparently line-height puts half the extra space above and half below the line, so the very top of the song gets scrunched. I could deal with that programmatically if I have to, but unless I find a way to place the chords correctly, there isn't much point in using this method.

So, the basic problem is that "position-relative" seems to be always vertically relative to the beginning of the current paragraph instead of the spot where the <span> actually is. Horizontally, it seems to follow the text flow nicely, but not vertically.

How can I get spans with "position:relative" to follow the vertical position of lines when they wrap? Or is there another way to accomplish the task with a different CSS?

A: You can consider using ruby.

http://www.w3.org/TR/css3-ruby/

It seems a more natural fit than trying to match spans.

Firefox has a (free) extension that supports ruby mark up. Opera (so far as I know) does not.

There is a blunt object workaround providing ruby support through CSS.

You can try this code:

```
<!DOCTYPE html PUBLIC "-//W3C//DTD XHTML 1.0
Transitional//EN" "http://www.w3.org/TR/xhtml1/DTD/xhtml1-
transitional.dtd">
<html xmlns: "http://www.w3.org/1999/xhtml">
<head>
<meta http-equiv: "Content-Type" content: "text/html;
charset: iso-8859-1" />
<title>Untitled Document</title>
<link href:
"http://web.nickshanks.com/stylesheets/ruby.css" rel:
"stylesheet"/>
</head>

<body>
  <ruby>
    <rb>When</rb>
    <rt>D</rt>
  </ruby>
  the music
  <ruby>
    <rb>fades</rb>
    <rt>A/C#</rt>
  </ruby>
  , all is stripped
  <ruby>
    <rb>away</rb>
    <rt>Em</rt>
  </ruby>

</body>
</html>
```

Another suggestion is to just use CSS to style it.

```
<!DOCTYPE html PUBLIC "-//W3C//DTD XHTML 1.0
Transitional//EN" "http://www.w3.org/TR/xhtml1/DTD/xhtml1-
transitional.dtd">
```

```
<html xmlns: "http://www.w3.org/1999/xhtml">
<head>
<meta http-equiv: "Content-Type" content: "text/html;
charset: iso-8859-1" />
<title>Untitled Document</title>
<link href:
"http://web.nickshanks.com/stylesheets/ruby.css" rel:
"stylesheet"/>
<style type: "text/css">ruby rt {text-align:left;
color:red; margin-left:20px; font-size:0.9em;}</style>
</head>
<body>
  <ruby>
    <rb>When the music </rb><rt>D</rt>
    </ruby>
    <ruby>
    <rb>fades, all is stripped
</rb><rt>A/C#</rt></ruby><ruby><rb>away</rb><rt>Em</rt></ru
by>
</body>
</html>
```

Question 74: Floating Text (div) is Causing Problems

I've come up with a design in Fireworks which I've tried to implement in XHTML and CSS.

Basically, there are two divs which contain "floating text." These elements have IDs of "floating_text1" and "floating_text2." I've set "floating_text1" to have an absolute position on the right side of the page and have been trying to get "floating_text2" to sit on the bottom of/or just below the purple navigation bar on the left side.

I'm having real difficulties with this and have been trying different things to achieve my aim. I thought I'd managed to sort it out by setting its position as relative and its z-index to 1 so that it overlays the navigation bar. This works okay in IE, but in FF it screws up my "Contact Us" page because for some reason, it has a large background which sits over the form elements due to the z-index. I have given the two floating text divs a pink background color just to highlight the problem.

By the way, I have only implemented the Home, The Teacher, and Contact Us pages. Home and The Teacher pages behave in a desirable way, but I think this is only because there is a lot more text on each of those pages, so it pushes "floating_text2" further down the page away from the navigation bar. I've tried removing "floating_text2" completely, but then the page height does strange things.

What is causing this and how can I rectify it so that it behaves consistently in both browsers?

A: You're right about the content. When there is enough content in the "div#content," you get your expected results because everything else is absolutely positioned, which does not attribute to the height of the parent container.

I suggest you rewrite your code to use floats instead of absolute positioning or enforce a minimum height on the element.

You do not need any positioning for floated elements. You would need positions only if you require it for reference points with the other elements that you might use absolute positioning on. You should look into float property.

Question 75: Background Images Not Showing in IE

Here is the layout:

http://81art.com/projects/atlanticrealestate/

It is both HTML and CSS validated. Mozilla plays along nicely with no problem.

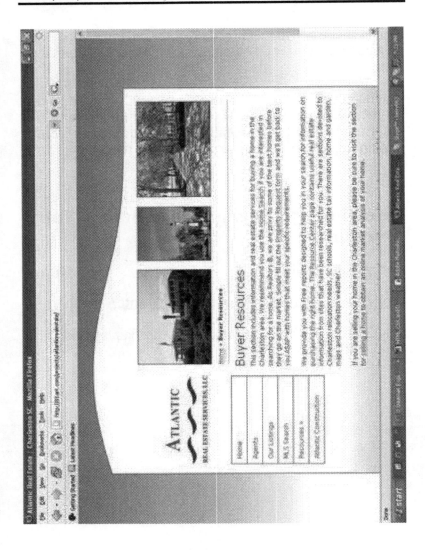

IE, on the other hand, is not showing some background images while others are fine.

This is an example of a working image:

```
#menuwrapper_bottom {
    background: url(../images/layout/menu_bottom.jpg)
```

```
bottom center no-repeat;
    width: 200px;
    height: 31px;
    }
```

Example of a similar image that is not working:

```
#menuwrapper {
    width: 180px;
    height: 200px;
    margin: 0 10px;
    background: url(../images/layout/logo.jpg) top center
no-repeat;
    padding: 125px 0 50px 0;
    }
```

Both of these examples are from:

http://81art.com/projects/atlanticrealestate/stylesheets/verticle_menu.css

Can you pinpoint what I am missing?

A: IE gets confused because the top part of the menu lies beneath the header images and breadcrumbs. I would suggest rewriting how the page is laid out. You can consider having two columns to begin with: left is navigation and right is header, breadcrumbs and content. It would show up how you want it to look.

Your "#container" is zero size high. Make sure you put a dummy element at the bottom of the floated elements (with clear both specified) inside the container to make it extend all the way down. Then, you'll probably also see the background.

Question 76: DIVS

I'm trying to get text to appear over an image.

My HTML:

```
<div style: "contentContainer" align: "center">
  <img src: "Images/textfield.gif">
  <div style: "content" align: "center" id: "Main">
    TEXT GOES HERE!
  </div>
</div>
```

My CSS:

```
#contentContainer {
    position: absolute;
    width: 770px;
    top: 10px;
    z-index: 1;
}

#content {
    position: absolute;
    top: -700px;
    width: 760px;
    height: 760px;
    overflow: auto;
    padding: 5px;
    z-index: 10;
}
```

When I load the page, the text appears at the bottom of the page under "textfield.gif."

Where have I gone wrong?

A: Just make the image a background image for the container div, then you won't have to mess with the positioning of the content div (well not as much as you normally would):

```
Code:

#contentContainer {
    position: absolute;
    width: 770px;
```

```
    top: 10px;
    z-index: 1;
    background:url(./images/textfield.gif) top left no-
repeat;
}
#content {
    position: absolute;
    top: -700px;
    width: 760px;
    height: 760px;
    overflow: auto;
    padding: 5px;
    z-index: 10;
}

<div style: "contentContainer" align: "center">
  <img src: "Images/textfield.gif">
  <div style: "content" align: "center" id: "Main">
    TEXT GOES HERE!
  </div>
</div>
```

Now the text is in the right place and "textfield.gif" isn't showing up at all. There are two things that come to mind that may be causing this:

1. Your content div has a background defined, and as such is overwriting what is behind it.
2. You have your CSS in an external file that is embedded in a CSS directory. If this is the case, your directory reference to the image is no longer valid (with respect to the CSS file). You will have to go down a directory to get to the "root" and then up to the image. Like so: background:url(../images/textfield.gif) top left "no-repeat;".

In your CSS, you assume that these divs have an id of "contentContainer" and content. Style attribute exists to insert inline CSS styles to the element, not to give it a name. You name the element by giving it a class (if there will be more elements with the same style on the page) and referencing it with a dot in CSS (.myClass) or an id (if the element appears only once on the page) and referencing it with a hash (#myId).

So, since in your case, you are expecting your HTML in your CSS to have certain ids, I suggest you add them:

```
Code:

<div id: "contentContainer" align: "center">
  <div id: "content" align: "center">
  </div>
</div>
```

Last but not least, check why your navigation is handled via AJAX.

Question 77: Div Alignment and FireFox

I have a div:

Code:

```
<div style: "text-align: right; width: 400px;">
   blah
</div>
```

This works for alignment on IE, but not in FireFox.

Can you tell me the proper way to do this with style/CSS?

A: Since you say "div alignment" in your title, I gather you want to align the div to the right. Not just text within the div, which is what you're doing right now. So you should try:

Code:

```
<div style: "margin-right: 0; margin-left: auto; width:
400px;">
   blah
</div>
```

Also style: "float: right" will work with a slightly different behavior. It depends what you want to use it for.

Question 78: DIV Floating Issues

This following page works in Firefox, but not in Internet Explorer.

Is there anyway I can make it work with both browsers?

CSS:

```
/**
 * Main Style
 */
body,td,th,div {
    font: 12px Arial, Helvetica, sans-serif;
    color: #000000;
}
body {
    background-color: #E1D4C0;
    margin: 0px;
}

/**
 * DIV Header Style
 */
#head {
    background: #143771 url(headbg.gif) repeat-x left top;
    height: 70px;
    text-align: center;
    padding: 0px;
    clear: both;
}
#head #hold {
    margin: auto;
    width: 850px;
    clear: both;
    padding: 0px;
}
#head #hold #left {
    float: left;
    width: 50px;
    background: url(headl.gif);
    height: 70px;
    clear: left;
}
#head #hold #middle {
    width: 742px;
    background: url(head.gif) no-repeat left top;
    height: 68px;
    margin-right: 50px;
    margin-left: 50px;
    text-align: left;
```

```
        vertical-align: top;
        color: #FFFFFF;
        padding: 2px 4px;
}
#head #hold #right {
        background: url(headr.gif) no-repeat right top;
        height: 70px;
        width: 50px;
        float: right;
        clear: right;
}
```

HTML:

```
<!DOCTYPE html PUBLIC "-//W3C//DTD XHTML 1.0
Transitional//EN" "http://www.w3.org/TR/xhtml1/DTD/xhtml1-
transitional.dtd">
<html xmlns: "http://www.w3.org/1999/xhtml">
<head>
<meta http-equiv: "Content-Type" content: "text/html;
charset: iso-8859-1" />
<link href: "img/style.css" rel: "stylesheet" type:
"text/css" />
<title>Flock</title>
</head>

<body>
<div id: "head">
  <div id: "hold">
    <div id: "left"></div>
    <div id: "right"></div>
    <div id: "middle"><img src: "img/logo.gif" width: "178"
height: "70" /></div>
  </div>
</div>
<div id: "divider"></div>
<div id: "content">
  <div id: "hold">
    <p>Content.</p>
  </div>
</div>
</body>
</html>
```

I only gave the header CSS code because that is the only part I'm having the problem with.

A: That's a good layout you have there. I can't see what IE is objecting to, but I have two suggestions.

1. Try giving various divs "position:relative; ". That sometimes clears mystery in IE bugs.

2. You can get rid of "div#left" and "div#right." Instead, make an 850px wide background with the left and right shadows on it (the bit that'll end up behind "div#middle" can be a plain color) and make it the background for "div#hold."

Alternatively, put another nested div inside "div#hold," say "div#hold2," then give "div#hold headl.gif" as a background image, and "div#hold2 headr.gif" each background-positioned into the relevant corner. Either way, getting rid of those two floating divs will simplify your markup and may get IE to behave.

Question 79: Div Pushing Another

I'm having difficulty getting one div not to push another down and away.

The top is where "Established 1866" is, it should be centered and the address section should remain more or less vertically centered and to the right. But it's getting pushed down.

How can I make this right?

A: Put that information grouped into 1 div, and then float that div to the right. Additionally, you will have to put the HTML for that div before the "established" HTML.

Question 80: FireFox Doesn't Break; Lines and Gaps in IE Around Images

I have two problems regarding the site.

1. One of my pages has a 3 column layout, and in Firefox only the paragraph in the middle column does not seem to recognize the </br> tag as there are no line breaks appearing and the text is showing as one block.

2. In IE, a gap appears between my images and my DIV. Both the DIV and Image are set to the same height and width.

Here is the XHTML:

```
<div id: "leftside">
  <div class: "left1"> </div>
  <div class: "left2"> <img src: "../images/countdrug.jpg"
```

```
height: "100" width: "100" alt: "drug1" /> </div>
   <div class: "left3"> </div>
   <div class: "left4"> <img src: "../images/countdrug.jpg"
height: "100" width: "100" alt: "drug2" /> </div>
   <div class: "left5"> </div>
   </div>

<div id: "rightside"><img src: "../images/map.gif" height:
"320" width: "320" alt: "map to cleary's pharmacy"
/>  </div>

 <div id: "anchorcontentd">
    <div class: "contentd">

    <h1> Contact Details</h1>
    <p>
    Address: Strand Road Portmarnock</br>
    Co. Dublin.
    </br>
    Telephone: +353 1 8461466
    </br>
    Facsimile: +353 1 8461326
    </br>
    e-mail:<a href: "mailto:me.ie"><img class: "middle"
src: "images/sendit.gif" width: "200" height: "20" alt:
"email us"/> </a>
    </p>

    <h1> Business Hours </h1>

    <p>
    Monday - Friday: 9.30am - 8.00pm
    </br>
    Saturday: 9.30am - 6.00pm
    </br>
    Sunday & Bank Holidays: 12.00am - 1.30pm
    </p>

      </div>
  </div>
```

And here is the CSS:

```
#leftside{
    float: left;
    width: 150px;
    height: 340px;
    background-color: #0000ff;}

.left1 {
    margin-left:10px;
    width:102px;
    height:10px;
```

```
    border-left: 1px solid #ffffff;}

.left2 {
    margin-left:10px;
    height:100px;
    width:100px;
    border-top: 1px solid #ffffff;
    border-left: 1px solid #ffffff;
    border-right: 1px solid #ffffff;}

.left3 {
    margin-left:10px;
    height:10px;
    width:101px;
    border-right: 1px solid #ffffff;
    border-top: 1px solid #ffffff;}

.left4 {
    margin-left:10px;
    height:100px;
    width:100px;
    border: 1px solid #ffffff;}

.left5 {
    margin-left:10px;
    width:102px;
    height:10px;
    border-left: 1px solid #ffffff;}

#rightside{
    float: right;
    width: 320px;
    height: 340px;}

#anchorcontentd{
    margin: 0px 320px 0px 150px;
    height: 340px;
    border-right: 1px solid #0000ff;}


.contentd{
    padding: 10px 10px 10px 10px;
    min-height: 340px;
    height: 340px;
    font-face: arial;
    font-size: 15px;}
```

What can I do to make this right?

A: For the line breaks, the tag should be <br />, not
</br>.

IE is a little weird when it comes to white space around images. Take the white space out of your code for the images and it should fix the issue.

Question 81: White Space between Border and Element

I'm trying to put a 3px white space between the border of one of my divs and the border. If it's not possible, should I just put a div around it with 3px margin, with the border instead?

I'm giving my div a background color, but I want white space between it and a border. Is it possible?

A: You'll need two divs to do that:

Code:

```
<div class: "double"><div>
Content goes here!
</div></div>
Then you can style it like this:

div.outer {
    border: 1px solid red;
    background: white;
    padding: 3px;
}

div.outer div {
    background: red;
}
```

The CSS should be:

```
div.double {
    border: 1px solid red;
    background: white;
    padding: 3px;
}

div.double div {
    background: red;
}
```

Question 82: Pages Not Being Displayed Properly Across Browsers

Here's my link:

http://home.bellsouth.net/p/pwp-dlfmedia_

It displays properly in Explorer, but in Opera and Firefox, the paragraphs don't have spaces between them. In Netscape, the paragraphs don't have spaces, and some of the styles applied to the <div id: "sidebar"> are not displaying properly. Also, the frames in the source from that link are not in my code, Bellsouth added that. Layout is controlled by CSS. This is just a test site.

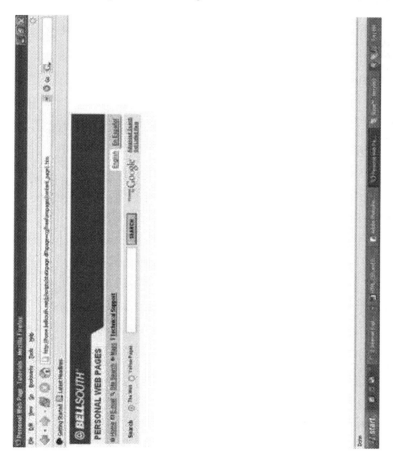

What's wrong in my CSS and how can I fix it so that it displays similar to Explorer?

A: This is your paragraph declaration in CSS:

```
p {
color:#666666;
font-family:Verdana, Arial, Helvetica, sans-serif;
font-size:12px;
margin: auto 40px auto 25px;
}
```

You're putting auto margins on the top and bottom of the paragraph. I suppose IE doesn't know what to do with that, so it reverts to default values.

FF is probably similarly confused but it reverts to 0. If you put a decent margin, like 1em, you should stop seeing the problem.

DHTML: Frequently Asked Questions

Question 83: DHTML Definition

What is DHTML?

A: It is a combination of HTML, Cascading Style Sheet (CSS), CSS-Positioning-P, and JavaScript. A typical DHTML application is made up of some elements created with standard HTML codes, formatted with Cascading Style Sheets, and most likely positioned on the Web page with CSS-P, that are then manipulated with JavaScript.

Question 84: Advantage of DHTML

What is the advantage of using DHTML?

A: It enhances your existing HTML pages with scripting to make your user interface more interactively.

Question 85: DHTML and CSS

Is DHTML in any way related to CSS?

A: CSS is one of the backbones of DHTML which allows you to separate the formatting of your pages from the content. You can change all or most of the elements on your page, with little to no scripting. One example is to make layers appear and disappear.

Question 86: Supporting browsers of DHTML

Which browsers support DHTML?

A: Both Microsoft and Netscape support Dynamic HTML in their 4.0 versions. However, IE supports much more of DOM which gives a wider range of tools to make use of.

Question 87: Substitute to JavaScript

Can DHTML be a substitute to JavaScript?

A: It can't replace JavaScript because it is its superset, which means that without JavaScript, there is no DHTML. There should be a combination of JavaScript and CSS to make the pages more dynamic.

Question 88: Learning DHTML

Does it help to have a background in HTML in learning DHTML?

A: It helps a lot along with having knowledge in CSS and JavaScript. You can refer to the following website for examples:

http://www.dhtmlshock.com/resources.asp

Question 89: HTML Tools Working with DHTML

Can a current HTML tools work with DHTML?

A: Almost all tools that create HTML allow a manual addition of DHTML to your pages. Macromedia Dreamweaver or Dreamweaver Ultradev are highly recommended and can be used as an authoring tool.

Question 90: Older browser

Can I use an older browser to view a DHTML-based page?

A: It depends on what was done with the DHTML and how it was coded. If the script was written well, it should fail without any errors. You can use a browser sniffer to do that and write a separate code for each of the major browsers.

Question 91: Document Object Model

How is Document Object Model related to DHTML?

A: The Document Object Model defines the properties and methods for the different elements on an HTML page. When you modify the properties of the HTML elements on a page via client-side scripting (e.g., using JavaScript) you can make your page interactive.

Question 92: Prevent Replication

Can I prevent others from copying my DHTML code?

A: You can't prevent others from doing that. There is no method to protect your codes including DHTML scripts.

Question 93: "Fading Text Scroller" On Mouse Over

I was wondering if it is possible to make the "Fading Text Scroller" pause whenever the mouse pointer is on the scrolling text.

A: You can use the DHTML Menu tool to realize the effect that you want.

Question 94: DHTML Menu

I'm new to DHTML and have been experimenting with creating a drop down menu. I have the menu of how I want it to look. The problem is, the user would have to click on the heading before the drop down menu appears. I would like to know what code can help and where I should put it so that the drop down menu appears as the user hovers over the heading, rather than wait for it to be clicked on first.

Code:

```
<!DOCTYPE html PUBLIC "-//W3C//DTD XHTML 1.0
Transitional//EN" "http://www.w3.org/TR/xhtml1/DTD/xhtml1-
transitional.dtd">
<html xmlns: "http://www.w3.org/1999/xhtml">
<head>
<meta http-equiv: "Content-Type" content: "text/html;
charset= iso-8859-1" />
<!-- TemplateBeginEditable name: "doctitle" -->
<title>untitled</title>
<!-- TemplateEndEditable --><script language: "JavaScript"
type: "text/javascript">
var objNavMenu :  null;
var prevObjNavMenu :  null;
var prevObjDropMenu :  null;
var numDropMenu :  7;
////// link styles
var bgLinkColor :  '#000000';
var bgLinkHover :  '#000000'
var bgLinkActive :  '#000000'
var linkColor :  '#ffffff'
var linkHover :  '#990000'
var linkActive :  '#ffffff'

var isIE :  null;
if (navigator.appName.indexOf('Microsoft Internet
Explorer') !:  -1) isIE: 1;

function initDropMenu () {
document.onclick : hideDropMenu;
for (i: 1; i<: numDropMenu; i++) {
menuName : 'dropMenu' + i;
navName : 'navMenu' + i;
objDropMenu :  document.getElementById(menuName);
objNavMenu :  document.getElementById(navName);
objDropMenu.style.visibility : 'hidden';
objNavMenu.onmouseover : menuHover;
objNavMenu.onmouseout : menuOut;
```

```
objNavMenu.onclick :   showDropMenu;
}
objNavMenu :  null;
return;
}

function menuHover(e) {
document.onclick :  null;
hoverObjNavMenu :  document.getElementById(this.id);
if (hoverObjNavMenu !:  objNavMenu) {
hoverObjNavMenu.style.color :  linkHover;
hoverObjNavMenu.style.backgroundColor :  bgLinkHover;
}
}

function menuOut (e) {
document.onclick :  hideDropMenu;
outObjNavMenu :  document.getElementById(this.id);
if (outObjNavMenu !:  objNavMenu) {
outObjNavMenu.style.color :  linkColor;
outObjNavMenu.style.backgroundColor :  bgLinkColor;
}
}

function showDropMenu(e) {
menuName :  'drop' + this.id.substring(3,this.id.length);
objDropMenu :  document.getElementById(menuName);
if (prevObjDropMenu : :  objDropMenu) {
hideDropMenu();
return;
}
if (prevObjDropMenu !:  null) hideDropMenu();
objNavMenu :  document.getElementById(this.id);
if ((prevObjNavMenu !:  objNavMenu ) || (prevObjDropMenu :
:  null)) {
objNavMenu.style.color :  linkActive;
objNavMenu.style.backgroundColor :  bgLinkActive;
}

if (objDropMenu) {
xPos :  objNavMenu.offsetParent.offsetLeft +
objNavMenu.offsetLeft;
yPos :  objNavMenu.offsetParent.offsetTop +
objNavMenu.offsetParent.offsetHeight;
if (isIE) {
yPos -:  1;
xPos -:  6;
}
objDropMenu.style.left :  xPos + 'px';
objDropMenu.style.top :  yPos + 'px';
objDropMenu.style.visibility :  'visible';
prevObjDropMenu :  objDropMenu;
prevObjNavMenu :  objNavMenu;
}
```

```
}

function hideDropMenu() {
document.onclick : null;
if (prevObjDropMenu) {
prevObjDropMenu.style.visibility :   'hidden';
prevObjDropMenu : null;
prevObjNavMenu.style.color : linkColor;
prevObjNavMenu.style.backgroundColor : bgLinkColor;
}
objNavMenu : null;
}

</script>
<style type: "text/css" media: "screen">
<!--
body {
margin: 0px;
padding: 0px;
}

#page {
margin: 10px;
}

#menuBar {
color: #000000;
font-size: xx-small;
font-family: Verdana, Arial, Helvetica, sans-serif;
font-weight: bold;
text-align: left;
text-transform: capitalize;
display: block;
margin-bottom: 5px;
position: relative;
top: 0px;
left: 0;
right: 0px;
width: 99%;
overflow: hidden;
vertical-align: middle;
border: solid 1px #000000;
background-color: #000000;
font-style: normal;
line-height: normal;
font-variant: normal;
}

.menuHeader {
color: #ffffff;
text-decoration: none;
white-space: nowrap;
cursor: pointer;
```

```
padding: 5px;
margin: 0px;
padding-right: 15px;
display: inline;
position: relative;
border-right: 1px solid #000000;
}

a.menuLink {
display: block;
padding: 2px 5px;
border-top: 1px solid #cccccc;
font-family: Verdana, Arial, Helvetica, sans-serif;
font-size: 9pt;
font-style: normal;
line-height: normal;
font-weight: normal;
font-variant: normal;
color: #FFFFFF;
}

a.menuLink:link {
color: #ffffff;
text-decoration: none
}

a.menuLink:visited {
color: #000000;
text-decoration: none
}

a.menuLink:hover {
color: #ffffff;
background-color: #CCCCCC;
text-decoration: none
}

a.menuLink:active {
color: #ffffff;
text-decoration: none;
background-color: #cc0000;
}

.menuDrop {
color: #FFFFFF;
font-size: xx-small;
font-family: Verdana, Arial, Helvetica, sans-serif;
background-color: #666666;
background-repeat: repeat;
visibility: hidden;
margin: 0;
padding: 0;
position: absolute;
z-index: 1000;
```

```
top: 60px;
left: 0;
width: 125px;
height: auto;
border-style: solid;
border-width: 0 1px 1px;
border-color: #003365;
font-style: normal;
line-height: normal;
font-weight: normal;
font-variant: normal;
}
.copyright {
font-family: Verdana, Arial, Helvetica, sans-serif;
font-size: xx-small;
font-style: normal;
line-height: normal;
font-weight: normal;
font-variant: normal;
color: #FFFFFF;
}
.content { font-family: Verdana, Arial, Helvetica, sans-
serif;
font-size: 9pt;
font-style: normal;
line-height: normal;
color: #000000;
font-weight: normal;
}
.sub_heading { color: #990000;
font-family: Verdana, Arial, Helvetica, sans-serif;
font-size: 9pt;
font-style: normal;
line-height: normal;
font-weight: normal;
font-variant: normal;
}
.form_text {font-family: Verdana, Arial, Helvetica, sans-
serif;
font-size: 10px;
}
.title_heading { font-size: 10pt;
font-family: Verdana, Arial, Helvetica, sans-serif;
color: #990000;
font-style: normal;
line-height: normal;
font-weight: bold;
font-variant: normal;
}
a:link {
color: #999999;
}
a:hover {
color: #990000;
```

```
}
a:visited {
color: #999999;
}

-->
</style>

<!-- TemplateBeginEditable name: "head" --><!--
TemplateEndEditable -->
</head>

<body bgcolor: "#ffffff" onload: "initDropMenu()">
<div id: "dropMenu1" class: "menuDrop">
<a class: "menuLink" href: "#" onfocus:
"if(this.blur)this.blur();">Link 1</a>
<a class: "menuLink" href: "#" onfocus:
"if(this.blur)this.blur();">Link 2</a>
<a class: "menuLink" href: "#" onfocus:
"if(this.blur)this.blur();">Link 3</a>
</div>

<div id: "dropMenu2" class: "menuDrop">
<a class: "menuLink" href: "#" onfocus:
"if(this.blur)this.blur();">Link 1</a>
<a class: "menuLink" href: "#" onfocus:
"if(this.blur)this.blur();">Link 2</a>
<a class: "menuLink" href: "#" onfocus:
"if(this.blur)this.blur();">Link 3</a>
</div>

<div id: "dropMenu3" class: "menuDrop">
<a class: "menuLink" href: "#" onfocus:
"if(this.blur)this.blur();">Link 1</a>
<a class: "menuLink" href: "#" onfocus:
"if(this.blur)this.blur();">Link 2</a>
<a class: "menuLink" href: "#" onfocus:
"if(this.blur)this.blur();">Link 3</a>
</div>

<div id: "dropMenu4" class: "menuDrop">
<a class: "menuLink" href: "#" onfocus:
"if(this.blur)this.blur();">Link 1</a>
<a class: "menuLink" href: "#" onfocus:
"if(this.blur)this.blur();">Link 2</a>
<a class: "menuLink" href: "#" onfocus:
"if(this.blur)this.blur();">Link 3</a>
</div>

<div id: "dropMenu5" class: "menuDrop">
<a class: "menuLink" href: "#" onfocus:
"if(this.blur)this.blur();">Link 1</a>
<a class: "menuLink" href: "#" onfocus:
"if(this.blur)this.blur();">Link 2</a>
```

```
<a class: "menuLink" href: "#" onfocus:
"if(this.blur)this.blur();">Link 3</a>
</div>

<div id: "dropMenu6" class: "menuDrop">
<a class: "menuLink" href: "#" onfocus:
"if(this.blur)this.blur();">Link 1</a>
<a class: "menuLink" href: "#" onfocus:
"if(this.blur)this.blur();">Link 2</a>
<a class: "menuLink" href: "#" onfocus:
"if(this.blur)this.blur();">Link 3</a>
</div>

<div id: "dropMenu7" class: "menuDrop">
<a class: "menuLink" href: "#" onfocus:
"if(this.blur)this.blur();">Link 1</a>
<a class: "menuLink" href: "#" onfocus:
"if(this.blur)this.blur();">Link 2</a>
<a class: "menuLink" href: "#" onfocus:
"if(this.blur)this.blur();">Link 3</a>
</div>

<table width: "800" border: "0" id: "page">
<tr>
<th width: "1088" height: "0" bgcolor: "#FFFFFF" scope:
"col"><div align: "left">
<div id: "menuBar">
<div id: "navMenu1" class: "menuHeader">HOME</div>
<div id: "navMenu2" class: "menuHeader">HEADING 1</div>
<div id: "navMenu3" class: "menuHeader">HEADING 2</div>
<div id: "navMenu4" class: "menuHeader">HEADING 3</div>
<div id: "navMenu5" class: "menuHeader">HEADING 4</div>
<div id: "navMenu6" class: "menuHeader">HEADING 5</div>
<div id: "navMenu7" class: "menuHeader">HEADING 6</div>
</div>
</div></th>
</tr>
</table>
</body>
</html>
```

How can I do that?

A: I think all you need to change is line 32, depending on how you count.

It's in:

```
function initDropMenu ()
...
```

```
objNavMenu.onmouseover :   menuHover;
objNavMenu.onmouseout :   menuOut;
objNavMenu.onclick :  showDropMenu;
```

Change it to:

```
objNavMenu.onmouseover :   showDropMenu;
objNavMenu.onmouseout :   menuOut;
objNavMenu.onclick :  showDropMenu;
```

All you are changing is the "onmouseover" command.

Events, Collections, Constants, Methods, Properties, and Objects Defined by DHTML

Question 95: Events

Can you give me the "events" exposed by the DHTML Object Model and define them?

A: The following are the EVENTS:

onabort: Fires when the user aborts the download of an image.

onactivate: Fires when the object is set as the active element.

onafterprint: Fires on the object immediately after its associated document prints or previews for printing.

onafterupdate: Fires on a databound object after successfully updating the associated data in the data source object.

onbeforeactivate: Fires immediately before the object is set as the active element.

onbeforecopy: Fires on the source object before the selection is copied to the system clipboard.

onbeforecut: Fires on the source object before the selection is deleted from the document.

onbeforedeactivate: Fires immediately before the activeElement is changed from the current object to another object in the parent document.

onbeforeeditfocus: Fires before an object contained in an editable element enters a UI-activated state or when an editable container object is control selected.

onbeforepaste: Fires on the target object before the selection is pasted from the system clipboard to the document.

onbeforeprint: Fires on the object before its associated document prints or previews for printing.

onbeforeunload: Fires prior to a page being unloaded.

onbeforeupdate: Fires on a databound object before updating the associated data in the data source object.

onblur: Fires when the object loses the input focus.

onbounce: Fires when the behavior property of the marquee object is set to "alternate" and the contents of the marquee reach one side of the window.

oncellchange: Fires when data changes in the data provider.

onchange: Fires when the contents of the object or selection have changed.

onclick: Fires when the user clicks the left mouse button on the object.

oncontextmenu: Fires when the user clicks the right mouse button in the client area, opening the context menu.

oncontrolselect: Fires when the user is about to make a control selection of the object.

oncopy: Fires on the source element when the user copies the object or selection, adding it to the system clipboard.

oncut: Fires on the source element when the object or selection is removed from the document and added to the system clipboard.

ondataavailable: Fires periodically as data arrives from data source objects that asynchronously transmit their data.

ondatasetchanged: Fires when the data set exposed by a data source object changes.

ondatasetcomplete: Fires to indicate that all data is available from the data source object.

ondblclick: Fires when the user double-clicks the object.

ondeactivate: Fires when the activeElement is changed from the current object to another object in the parent document.

ondrag: Fires on the source object continuously during a drag operation.

ondragend: Fires on the source object when the user releases the mouse at the close of a drag operation.

ondragenter: Fires on the target element when the user drags the object to a valid drop target.

ondragleave: Fires on the target object when the user moves the mouse out of a valid drop target during a drag operation.

ondragover: Fires on the target element continuously while the user drags the object over a valid drop target.

ondragstart: Fires on the source object when the user starts to drag a text selection or selected object.

ondrop: Fires on the target object when the mouse button is released during a drag-and-drop operation.

onerror: Fires when an error occurs during object loading.

onerrorupdate: Fires on a databound object when an error occurs while updating the associated data in the data source object.

onfilterchange: Fires when a visual filter changes state or completes a transition.

onfinish: Fires when marquee looping is complete.

onfocus: Fires when the object receives focus.

onfocusin: Fires for an element just prior to setting focus on that element.

onfocusout: Fires for the current element with focus immediately after moving focus to another element.

onhelp: Fires when the user presses the F1 key while the browser is the active window.

onkeydown: Fires when the user presses a key.

onkeypress: Fires when the user presses an alphanumeric key.

onkeyup: Fires when the user releases a key.

onlayoutcomplete: Fires when the print or print preview layout process finishes filling the current LayoutRect object with content from the source document.

onload: Fires immediately after the browser loads the object.

onlosecapture: Fires when the object loses the mouse capture.

onmousedown: Fires when the user clicks the object with either mouse button.

onmouseenter: Fires when the user moves the mouse pointer into the object.

onmouseleave: Fires when the user moves the mouse pointer outside the boundaries of the object.

onmousemove: Fires when the user moves the mouse over the object.

onmouseout: Fires when the user moves the mouse pointer outside the boundaries of the object.

onmouseover: Fires when the user moves the mouse pointer into the object.

onmouseup: Fires when the user releases a mouse button while the mouse is over the object.

onmousewheel: Fires when the wheel button is rotated.

onmove: Fires when the object moves.

onmoveend: Fires when the object stops moving.

onmovestart: Fires when the object starts to move.

onpaste: Fires on the target object when the user pastes data, transferring the data from the system clipboard to the document.

onpropertychange: Fires when a property changes on the object.

onreadystatechange: Fires when the state of the object has changed.

onreset: Fires when the user resets a form.

onresize: Fires when the size of the object is about to change.

onresizeend: Fires when the user finishes changing the dimensions of the object in a control selection.

onresizestart: Fires when the user begins to change the dimensions of the object in a control selection.

onrowenter: Fires to indicate that the current row has changed in the data source and new data values are available on the object.

onrowexit: Fires just before the data source control changes the current row in the object.

onrowsdelete: Fires when rows are about to be deleted from the recordset.

onrowsinserted: Fires just after new rows are inserted in the current recordset.

onscroll: Fires when the user repositions the scroll box in the scroll bar on the object.

onselect: Fires when the current selection changes.

onselectionchange: Fires when the selection state of a document changes.

onselectstart: Fires when the object is being selected.

onstart: Fires at the beginning of every loop of the marquee object.

onstop: Fires when the user clicks the Stop button or leaves the Web page.

onsubmit: Fires when a FORM is about to be submitted.

onunload: Fires immediately before the object is unloaded.

Question 96: Collections

Can you give me a list of the "collections" exposed by the DHTML Object Model and its definition?

A: The following is the list of collections:

all: Returns a reference to the collection of elements contained by the object.

anchors: Retrieves a collection of all a objects that have a name and/or id property. Objects in this collection are in HTML source order.

applets: Retrieves a collection of all applet objects in the document.

areas: Retrieves a collection of the area objects defined for the given map object.

attributes: Retrieves a collection of attributes of the object.

behaviorUrns: Returns a collection of Uniform Resource Name (URN) strings identifying the behaviors attached to the element.

blockFormats: Retrieves a collection of strings that specify the names of the available block format tags.

bookmarks: Returns a collection of Microsoft ActiveX Data Objects (ADO) bookmarks tied to the rows affected by the current event.

boundElements: Returns a collection of all elements on the page bound to a data set.

cells: Retrieves a collection of all cells in the table row or in the entire table.

childNodes: Retrieves a collection of HTML Elements and TextNode objects that are direct descendants of the specified object.

children: Retrieves a collection of DHTML Objects that are direct descendants of the object.

controlRange: A collection of elements returned by the createControlRange or createRange method.

elements: Retrieves a collection, in source order, of all controls in a given form. input type: image objects are excluded from the collection.

embeds: Retrieves a collection of all embed objects in the document.

filters: Retrieves the collection of filters that have been applied to the object.

fonts: Retrieves a collection of all the system-supported fonts.

forms: Retrieves a collection, in source order, of all form objects in the document.

frames: Retrieves a collection of all window objects defined by the given document or defined by the document associated with the given window.

images: Retrieves a collection, in source order, of img objects in the document.

imports: Retrieves a collection of all the imported style sheets defined for the respective styleSheet object.

links: Retrieves a collection of all **a** objects that specify the HREF property and all **area** objects in the document.

mimeTypes: Not currently implemented.

namespaces: Retrieves a collection of namespace objects.

options: Retrieves a collection of the option objects in a select object.

pages: Retrieves a collection of page objects, which represent @page rules in a **styleSheet**.

plugins: Retrieves a collection of all embed objects within the document.

rows: Retrieves a collection of tr (table row) objects from a table object.

rules: Retrieves a collection of rules defined in a style sheet.

scripts: Retrieves a collection of all script objects in the document.

styleSheets: Retrieves a collection of **styleSheet** objects representing the style sheets that correspond to each instance of a link or style object in the document.

tBodies: Retrieves a collection of all tBody objects in the table. Objects in this collection are in source order.

TextRange: Retrieves a collection of TextRange objects.

TextRectangle: A collection of TextRectangle objects returned by the getClientRects method.

Question 97: Constants

Can you give me the "constants" in the DHTML Object Model with its definition?

A: The following is the list of constants:

Color Table: Colors can be specified in HTML pages in two ways: by using a color name or by using numbers to denote an RGB color value. An RGB color value consists of three two-digit hexadecimal numbers specifying the intensity of the corresponding color.

Command Identifiers: Command identifiers specify an action to take on the given object.

Dialog Helper Character Sets: Return value from getCharset method.

HTTP Response Headers: The following list contains valid HTTP response headers. Use these headers to provide information about your HTML document in a meta tag, or to gather information about another document using HttpQueryInfo and QueryInfo.

Language Codes: The following table lists all the possible language codes used to specify various system settings.

Question 98: Methods

Can you give me the list of the "methods" exposed by the DHTML Object Model and its definition?

A: The following is the list of methods:

abort: Cancels the current HTTP request.

add: Creates a new namespace object and adds it to the collection.

add: Adds an element to the areas, controlRange, or options collection.

addBehavior: Attaches a behavior to the element.

AddChannel: Presents a dialog box that enables the user to either add the channel specified, or change the channel URL if it is already installed.

AddDesktopComponent: Adds a Web site or image to the Microsoft Active Desktop.

addElement: Adds an element to the controlRange collection.

AddFavorite: Prompts the user with a dialog box to add the specified URL to the Favorites list.

addImport: Adds a style sheet to the imports collection for the specified style sheet.

addPageRule: Creates a new page object for a style sheet.

addReadRequest: Adds an entry to the queue for read requests.

addRule: Creates a new rule for a style sheet.

AddSearchProvider: Adds a search provider to the registry.

alert: Displays a dialog box containing an application-defined message.

appendChild: Appends an element as a child to the object.

appendData: Adds a new character string to the end of the object.

applyElement: Makes the element either a child or parent of another element.

assign: Loads a new HTML document.

attachEvent: Binds the specified function to an event, so that the function gets called whenever the event fires on the object.

AutoCompleteSaveForm: Saves the specified form in the AutoComplete data store.

AutoScan: Attempts to connect to a Web server by passing the specified query through completion templates.

back: Loads a previous URL from the History list.

blur: Causes the element to lose focus and fires the onblur event.

BrandImageUri: Retrieves the Uniform Resource Identifier (URI) of the image used for branding.

ChooseColorDlg: Opens the system color-selection dialog box.

clear: Clears the contents of the selection.

clear: Not currently supported.

clearAttributes: Removes all attributes and values from the object.

clearData: Removes one or more data formats from the clipboard through dataTransfer or clipboardData object.

clearInterval: Cancels the interval previously started using the setInterval method.

clearRequest: Clears all requests in the read-requests queue to prepare for new profile-information requests.

clearTimeout: Cancels a time-out that was set with the setTimeout method.

click: Simulates a click by causing the onclick event to fire.

cloneNode: Copies a reference to the object from the document hierarchy.

close: Closes an output stream and forces the sent data to display.

close: Closes the current browser window or HTML Application (HTA).

collapse: Moves the insertion point to the beginning or end of the current range.

compareEndPoints: Compares an end point of a TextRange object with an end point of another range.

componentFromPoint: Returns the component located at the specified coordinates via certain events.

confirm: Displays a confirmation dialog box that contains an optional message as well as OK and Cancel buttons.

contains: Checks whether the given element is contained within the object.

createAttribute: Creates an attribute object with a specified name.

createCaption: Creates an empty caption element in the table.

createComment: Creates a comment object with the specified data.

createControlRange: Creates a controlRange collection of nontext elements.

createDocumentFragment: Creates a new document.

createElement: Creates an instance of the element for the specified tag.

createEventObject: Generates an event object for passing event context information when using the fireEvent method.

createPopup: Creates a popup window.

createRange: Creates a TextRange object from the current text selection, or a controlRange collection from a control selection.

createRangeCollection: Creates a TextRange object collection from the current selection.

createStyleSheet: Creates a style sheet for the document.

createTextNode: Creates a text string from the specified value.

createTextRange: Creates a TextRange object for the element.

createTFoot: Creates an empty tFoot element in the **table**.

createTHead: Creates an empty tHead element in the **table**.

CustomizeSettings: Saves the user settings from a "first run" page.

deleteCaption: Deletes the caption element and its contents from the table.

deleteCell: Removes the specified cell (td) from the table row, as well as from the cells collection.

deleteData: Removes a specified range of characters from the object.

deleteRow: Removes the specified row (tr) from the element and from the rows collection.

deleteTFoot: Deletes the tFoot element and its contents from the table.

deleteTHead: Deletes the tHead element and its contents from the table.

detachEvent: Unbinds the specified function from the event, so that the function stops receiving notifications when the event fires.

doImport: Dynamically imports an element behavior.

doReadRequest: Performs all requests located in the read-requests queue.

doScroll: Simulates a click on a scroll-bar component.

dragDrop: Initiates a drag event.

duplicate: Returns a duplicate of the TextRange.

elementFromPoint: Returns the element for the specified x and y coordinates.

empty: Cancels the current selection, sets the selection type to none, and sets the item property to null.

execCommand: Executes a command on the current document, current selection, or the given range.

execScript: Executes the specified script in the provided language.

expand: Expands the range so that partial units are completely contained.

findText: Searches for text in the document and positions the start and end points of the range to encompass the search string.

fireEvent: Fires a specified event on the object.

firstPage: Displays the first page of records in the data set to which the table is bound.

focus: Causes the element to receive the focus and executes the code specified by the onfocus event.

forward: Loads the next URL from the History list.

getAdjacentText: Returns the adjacent text string.

getAllResponseHeaders: Returns the complete list of response headers.

getAttribute: Retrieves the value of the specified attribute.

getAttribute: Returns the value of the named attribute from the userProfile object.

getAttributeNode: Retrieves an attribute objectreferenced by the attribute.nameproperty.

getBookmark: Retrieves a bookmark (opaque string) that can be used with moveToBookmark to return to the same range.

getBoundingClientRect: Retrieves an object that specifies the bounds of a collection of TextRectangle objects.

getCharset: Retrieves a Variant that specifies the character set of the specified font.

getClientRects: Retrieves a collection of rectangles that describes the layout of the contents of an object or range within the client. Each rectangle describes a single line.

getData: Retrieves the data in the specified format from the clipboard through the dataTransfer or clipboardData objects.

getElementById: Returns a reference to the first object with the specified value of the ID attribute.

getElementsByName: Retrieves a collection of objects based on the value of the NAME attribute.

getElementsByTagName: Retrieves a collection of objects based on the specified element name.

getExpression: Retrieves the expression for the given property.

getNamedItem: Retrieves an **attribute** specified with the **name** property using the attributes collection.

getResponseHeader: Returns the specified response header.

go: Loads a URL from the History list.

hasChildNodes: Returns a value that indicates whether the object has children.

hasFeature: Returns a value that indicates whether the object implements a specific Document Object Model (DOM) standard.

hasFocus: Retrieves the value indicating whether the object currently has focus.

hide: Closes the pop-up window.

ImportExportFavorites: Deprecated. Handles the importing and exporting of Microsoft Internet Explorer favorites.

inRange: Returns a value indicating whether one range is contained within another.

insertAdjacentElement: Inserts an element at the specified location.

insertAdjacentHTML: Inserts the given HTML text into the element at the location.

insertAdjacentText: Inserts the given text into the element at the specified location.

insertBefore: Inserts an element into the document hierarchy as a child node of a parent object.

insertCell: Creates a new cell in the table row (tr), and adds the cell to the cells collection.

insertData: Inserts a new character string in the object at a specified offset.

insertRow: Creates a new row (tr) in the table, and adds the row to the rows collection.

isEqual: Returns a value indicating whether the specified range is equal to the current range.

IsSubscribed: Retrieves a value indicating whether the client subscribes to the given channel.

item: Retrieves an attribute for an element from the attributes collection.

item: Retrieves an object from the bookmarks collection.

item: Retrieves an object from the controlRange collection.

item: Retrieves an object from the childNodes or children collection.

item: Retrieves a **namespace** object from the namespaces collection.

item: Retrieves an object from the pages collection.

item: Retrieves an object from the rules collection.

item: Retrieves an object from the all collection or various other collections.

item: Retrieves an object from the filters collection or various other collections.

item: Retrieves an object from the behaviorUrns collection.

Item: Retrieves a string that specifies the name of a block format tag.

javaEnabled: Returns whether Java is enabled.

lastPage: Displays the last page of records in the data set to which the table is bound.

mergeAttributes: Copies all read/write attributes to the specified element.

move: Collapses the given text range and moves the empty range by the given number of units.

moveBy: Moves the screen position of the window by the specified x and y offset values.

moveEnd: Changes the end position of the range.

moveRow: Moves a table row to a new position.

moveStart: Changes the start position of the range.

moveTo: Moves the screen position of the upper-left corner of the window to the specified *x* and *y* position.

moveToBookmark: Moves to a bookmark.

moveToElementText: Moves the text range so that the start and end positions of the range encompass the text in the given element.

moveToPoint: Moves the start and end positions of the text range to the given point.

namedItem: Retrieves an object or a collection from the specified collection.

namedRecordset: Retrieves the recordset object corresponding to the named data member from a data source object (DSO).

navigate: Loads the specified URL to the current window.

NavigateAndFind: Navigates to the specified URL and selects the specified text.
nextPage: Displays the next page of records in the data set to which the table is bound.

normalize: Merges adjacent TextNode objects to produce a normalized document object model.

open: This method works in two ways. It opens a document to collect the output of the write and writeln methods. In this case, only the first two parameters, *url* and *name* are used. When values for the additional parameters are specified, this method opens a window in the same way as the window.open method for the **window** object.

open: Opens a new window and loads the document specified by a given URL.

open: Assigns method, destination URL, and other optional attributes of a pending request.

parentElement: Retrieves the parent element for the given text range.

pasteHTML: Pastes HTML text into the given text range, replacing any previous text and HTML elements in the range.

PhishingEnabled: Determines whether Microsoft Phishing Filter is enabled.

previousPage: Displays the previous page of records in the data set to which the table is bound.

print: Prints the document associated with the window.

prompt: Displays a dialog box that prompts the user with a message and an input field.

queryCommandEnabled: Returns a Boolean value that indicates whether a specified command can be successfully executed using execCommand, given the current state of the document.

queryCommandIndeterm: Returns a Boolean value that indicates whether the specified command is in the indeterminate state.

queryCommandState: Returns a Boolean value that indicates the current state of the command.

queryCommandSupported: Returns a Boolean value that indicates whether the current command is supported on the current range.

queryCommandValue: Returns the current value of the document, range, or current selection for the given command.

recalc: Recalculates all dynamic properties in the current document.

refresh: Refreshes the content of the table. This might be necessary after a call to a method such as removeRule, when the page does not automatically reflow.

releaseCapture: Removes mouse capture from the object in the current document.

reload: Reloads the current page.

remove: Removes an element from the collection.

removeAttribute: Removes the given attribute from the object.

removeAttributeNode: Removes an attribute objectfrom the object.

removeBehavior: Detaches a behavior from the element.

removeChild: Removes a child node from the object.

removeExpression: Removes the expression from the specified property.

removeNamedItem: Removes an attribute specified with the name property from an element using the attributes collection.

removeNode: Removes the object from the document hierarchy.

removeRule: Deletes an existing style rule for the styleSheet object, and adjusts the index of the **rules** collection accordingly.

replace: Replaces the current document by loading another document at the specified URL.

replaceAdjacentText: Replaces the text adjacent to the element.

replaceChild: Replaces an existing child element with a new child element.

replaceData: Replaces a specified range of characters in the object with a new character string.

replaceNode: Replaces the object with another element.

reset: Simulates a mouse click on a reset button for the calling form.

resizeBy: Changes the current size of the window by the specified x- and y-offset.
resizeTo: Sets the size of the window to the specified width and height values.

RunOnceShown: Indicates that the "first run" page has been shown.

scroll: Causes the window to scroll to the specified x- and y-offset at the upper-left corner of the window.

scrollBy: Causes the window to scroll relative to the current scrolled position by the specified x- and y-pixel offset.

scrollIntoView: Causes the object to scroll into view, aligning it either at the top or bottom of the window.

scrollTo: Scrolls the window to the specified x- and y-offset.

select: Highlights the input area of a form element.

select: Makes the selection equal to the current object.

send: Sends an HTTP request to the server and receives a response.

setActive: Sets the object as active without setting focus to the object.

setAttribute: Sets the value of the specified attribute.

setAttributeNode: Sets an attribute objectnode as part of the object.

setCapture: Sets the mouse capture to the object belonging to the current document.

setData: Assigns data in a specified format to the dataTransfer or clipboardData object.

setEndPoint: Sets the endpoint of one range based on the endpoint of another range.

setExpression: Sets an expression for the specified object.

setInterval: Evaluates an expression each time a specified number of milliseconds has elapsed.

setNamedItem: Adds an attribute to an element using an attributes collection.

setRequestHeader: Adds custom HTTP headers to the request.

setTimeout: Evaluates an expression after a specified number of milliseconds has elapsed.

show: Displays the pop-up window on the screen.

ShowBrowserUI: Opens the specified browser dialog box.

showHelp: Displays a Help file. This method can be used with Microsoft HTML Help.

showModalDialog: Creates a modal dialog box that displays the specified HTML document.

showModelessDialog: Creates a modeless dialog box that displays the specified HTML document.

SkipRunOnce: Allows the user to select "first run" settings at a later time.

splitText: Divides a text node at the specified index.

SqmEnabled: Determines whether Software Quality Monitoring (SQM) is enabled.

start: Starts scrolling the marquee.

stop: Stops the marquee from scrolling.

submit: Submits the form.

substringData: Extracts a range of characters from the object.

swapNode: Exchanges the location of two objects in the document hierarchy.

tags: Retrieves a collection of objects that have the specified HTML tag name.

taintEnabled: Returns whether data tainting is enabled.

urns: Retrieves a collection of all objects to which a specified behavior is attached.

write: Writes one or more HTML expressions to a document in the specified window.

writeln: Writes one or more HTML expressions, followed by a carriage return, to a document in the specified window.

Question 99: Properties

Can you give me the list of the "properties" in the DHTML Object Model?

A: The following is the list of properties:

!important: Increases the weight or importance of a particular rule.

:active: Sets the style of an a element when the link is engaged or active.

:first-child: Applies one or more styles to any element that is the first child of its parent.

:first-letter: Applies one or more styles to the first letter of the object.

:first-line: Applies one or more styles to the first line of the object.

:hover: Sets the style of an element when the user hovers the mouse pointer over it.

:link: Sets the style of an a element when the link has not been visited recently.

:visited: Sets the style of an a element when the link has been visited recently.

@charset: Sets the character set for an external style sheet.

@font-face: Sets a font to embed in the HTML document.

@import: Imports an external style sheet.

@media: Sets the media types for a set of rules in a styleSheet object.

@page: Sets the dimensions, orientation, and margins of a page box in a styleSheet.

abbr: Sets or retrieves abbreviated text for the object.

accelerator: Sets or retrieves a string that indicates whether the object contains an accelerator key.

accept: Sets or retrieves a comma-separated list of content types.

acceptCharset: Sets or retrieves a list of character encodings for input data that must be accepted by the server processing the form.

accessKey: Sets or retrieves the accelerator key for the object.

action: Sets or retrieves the URL to which the form content is sent for processing.

activeElement: Retrieves the object that has the focus when the parent document has focus.

additive: Sets or retrieves a value that indicates whether the animation is additive with other animations.

align: Sets or retrieves how the object is aligned with adjacent text.

align: Sets or retrieves the alignment of the caption or legend.

align: Sets or retrieves a value that indicates the table alignment.

align: Sets or retrieves the alignment of the object relative to the display or table.

aLink: Sets or retrieves the color of all active links in the element.

alinkColor: Sets or retrieves the color of all active links in the document.

allowTransparency: Sets or retrieves whether the object can be transparent.

alt: Sets or retrieves a text alternative to the graphic.

altHTML: Sets the optional alternative HTML script to execute if the object fails to load.

altKey: Sets or retrieves a value that indicates the state of the ALT key.

altLeft: Sets or retrieves a value that indicates the state of the left ALT key.

appCodeName: Retrieves the code name of the browser.

APPLICATION: Indicates whether the content of the object is an HTML Application (HTA) and, therefore, exempt from the browser security model.

applicationName: Sets or retrieves the name of the HTML Application (HTA).

appMinorVersion: Retrieves the application's minor version value.

appName: Retrieves the name of the browser.

appVersion: Retrieves the platform and version of the browser.

archive: Sets or retrieves a character string that can be used to implement your own archive functionality for the object.

ATOMICSELECTION: Specifies whether the element and its contents must be selected as a whole, indivisible unit.

autocomplete: Sets or retrieves the status of AutoComplete for the object.

availHeight: Retrieves the height of the working area of the system's screen, excluding the Microsoft Windows taskbar.

availWidth: Retrieves the width of the working area of the system's screen, excluding the Windows taskbar.

axis: Sets or retrieves a comma-delimited list of conceptual categories associated with the object.

background: Sets or retrieves up to five separate background properties of the object.

background: Sets or retrieves the background picture tiled behind the text and graphics on the page.

background: Sets or retrieves the background picture tiled behind the text and graphics in the object.

backgroundAttachment: Sets or retrieves how the background image is attached to the object within the document.

backgroundColor: Sets or retrieves the color behind the content of the object.

backgroundImage: Sets or retrieves the background image of the object.

backgroundPosition: Sets or retrieves the position of the background of the object.

backgroundPositionX: Sets or retrieves the x-coordinate of the backgroundPosition property.

backgroundPositionY: Sets or retrieves the y-coordinate of the backgroundPosition property.

backgroundRepeat: Sets or retrieves how the backgroundImage property of the object is tiled.

balance: Sets or retrieves the value indicating how the volume of the background sound is divided between the left and right speakers.

Banner: Retrieves the Banner content of an entry in an Advanced Stream Redirector (ASX) file.

BannerAbstract: Retrieves the BannerAbstract content of an entry in an ASX file.

BaseHref: Retrieves a string of the URL where the object tag can be found. This is often the href of the document that the object is in, or the value set by a base element.

behavior: Sets or retrieves how the text scrolls in the marquee.

behavior: Sets or retrieves the location of the Introduction to DHTML Behaviors.

bgColor: Deprecated. Sets or retrieves the background color behind the object.

bgColor: Deprecated. Sets or retrieves a value that indicates the background color behind the object.

BGCOLOR: Sets the background color behind the object.

bgProperties: Sets or retrieves the properties of the background picture.

blockDirection: Retrieves a string value that indicates whether the content in the block element flows from left to right, or from right to left.

border: Sets or retrieves the properties to draw around the object.

border: Sets or retrieves the space between the frames, including the 3-D border.

border: Sets or retrieves the width of the border to draw around the object.

borderBottom: Sets or retrieves the properties of the bottom border of the object.

borderBottomColor: Sets or retrieves the color of the bottom border of the object.

borderBottomStyle: Sets or retrieves the style of the bottom border of the object.

borderBottomWidth: Sets or retrieves the width of the bottom border of the object.

borderCollapse: Sets or retrieves a value that indicates whether the row and cell borders of a table are joined in a single border or detached as in standard HTML.

borderColor: Sets or retrieves the border color of the object.

borderColor: Sets or retrieves the border color of the object.

borderColorDark Sets or retrieves the color for one of the two colors used to draw the 3-D border of the object.

borderColorLight: Sets or retrieves the color for one of the two colors used to draw the 3-D border of the object.

borderLeft: Sets or retrieves the properties of the left border of the object.

borderLeftColor: Sets or retrieves the color of the left border of the object.

borderLeftStyle: Sets or retrieves the style of the left border of the object.

borderLeftWidth: Sets or retrieves the width of the left border of the object.

borderRight: Sets or retrieves the properties of the right border of the object.

borderRightColor: Sets or retrieves the color of the right border of the object.

borderRightStyle: Sets or retrieves the style of the right border of the object.

borderRightWidth: Sets or retrieves the width of the right border of the object.

borderStyle: Sets or retrieves the style of the left, right, top, and bottom borders of the object.

borderTop: Sets or retrieves the properties of the top border of the object.

borderTopColor: Sets or retrieves the color of the top border of the object.

borderTopStyle: Sets or retrieves the style of the top border of the object.

borderTopWidth: Sets or retrieves the width of the top border of the object.

borderWidth: Sets or retrieves the width of the left, right, top, and bottom borders of the object.

bottom: Set or retrieves the bottom coordinate of the rectangle surrounding the object content.

bottom: Sets or retrieves the bottom position of the object in relation to the bottom of the next positioned object in the document hierarchy.

bottomMargin: Sets or retrieves the bottom margin of the entire body of the page.

boundingHeight: Retrieves the height of the rectangle that bounds the TextRange object.

boundingLeft: Retrieves the distance between the left edge of the rectangle that bounds the **TextRange** object and the left side of the object that contains the **TextRange**.

boundingTop: Retrieves the distance between the top edge of the rectangle that bounds the **TextRange** object and the top side of the object that contains the **TextRange**.

boundingWidth: Retrieves the width of the rectangle that bounds the TextRange object.

browserLanguage: Retrieves the current browser language.

bufferDepth: Sets or retrieves the number of bits per pixel used for colors in the off-screen bitmap buffer.

button: Sets or retrieves the mouse button pressed by the user.

cancelBubble: Sets or retrieves whether the current event should bubble up the hierarchy of event handlers.

canHaveChildren: Retrieves a value indicating whether the object can contain children.

canHaveHTML: Sets or retrieves the value indicating whether the object can contain rich HTML markup.

caption: Retrieves the caption object of the table.

cellIndex: Retrieves the position of the object in the cells collection of a row.

cellPadding: Sets or retrieves the amount of space between the border of the cell and the content of the cell.

cellSpacing: Sets or retrieves the amount of space between cells in a table.

ch: Sets or retrieves a value that you can use to implement your own ch functionality for the object.

charset: Sets or retrieves the character set used to encode the object.

checked: Sets or retrieves the state of the check box or radio button.

chOff: Sets or retrieves a value that you can use to implement your own chOff functionality for the object.

cite: Sets or retrieves reference information about the object.

classid: Sets or retrieves the class identifier for the object.

className: Sets or retrieves the class of the object.

clear: Sets or retrieves whether the object allows floating objects on its left side, right side, or both, so that the next text displays past the floating objects.

clear: Sets or retrieves the side on which floating objects are not to be positioned when a line break is inserted into the document.

clientHeight: Retrieves the height of the object including padding, but not including margin, border, or scroll bar.

clientLeft: Retrieves the distance between the offsetLeft property and the true left side of the client area.

clientTop: Retrieves the distance between the offsetTop property and the true top of the client area.

clientWidth: Retrieves the width of the object including padding, but not including margin, border, or scroll bar.

clientX: Sets or retrieves the x-coordinate of the mouse pointer's position relative to the client area of the window, excluding window decorations and scroll bars.

clientY: Sets or retrieves the y-coordinate of the mouse pointer's position relative to the client area of the window, excluding window decorations and scroll bars.

clip: Sets or retrieves which part of a positioned object is visible.

clipBottom: Retrieves the bottom coordinate of the object clipping region.

clipLeft: Retrieves the left coordinate of the object clipping region.

clipRight: Retrieves the right coordinate of the object clipping region.

clipTop: Retrieves the top coordinate of the object clipping region.

closed: Retrieves whether the referenced window is closed.

code: Sets or retrieves the URL of the file containing the compiled Java class.

codeBase: Sets or retrieves the URL of the component.

codeType: Sets or retrieves the Internet media type for the code associated with the object.

color: Sets or retrieves the color to be used by the object.

color: Sets or retrieves the color of the text of the object.

colorDepth: Retrieves the number of bits per pixel used for colors on the destination device or buffer.

cols: Sets or retrieves the frame widths of the object.

cols: Sets or retrieves the number of columns in the table.

cols: Sets or retrieves the width of the object.

colSpan: Sets or retrieves the number columns in the table that the object should span.

compact: Sets or retrieves a Boolean value indicating whether the list should be compacted by removing extra space between list objects.

compatMode: Retrieves a value that indicates whether standards-compliant mode is switched on for the object.

complete: Retrieves whether the object is fully loaded.

content: Sets or retrieves meta -information to associate with httpEquiv or name.

contentEditable: Sets or retrieves the string that indicates whether the user can edit the content of the object.

contentOverflow: Retrieves a value that indicates whether the document contains additional content after processing the current LayoutRect object.

contentWindow: Retrieves the window object of the specified frame or iframe.

cookie: Sets or retrieves the string value of a cookie.

cookieEnabled: Retrieves whether client-side persistent cookies are enabled in the browser. Persistent cookies are those that are stored on the client-side computer.

coords: Sets or retrieves the coordinates of the object.

Count: Retrieves the number of available block format tags.

cpuClass: Retrieves a string denoting the CPU class.

cssText: Sets or retrieves the persisted representation of the style rule.

ctrlKey: Sets or retrieves the state of the CTRL key.

ctrlLeft: Sets or retrieves the state of the left CTRL key.

cursor: Sets or retrieves the type of cursor to display as the mouse pointer moves over the object.

data: Sets or retrieves the value of a TextNode object.

data: Sets or retrieves the URL that references the data of the object.

dataFld: Sets or retrieves which field of a given data source, as specified by the dataSrc property, to bind to the specified object.

dataFld: Sets or retrieves the data column affected by the oncellchange event.

DATAFLD: Sets the field of a given data source for data binding.

dataFormatAs: Sets or retrieves how to render the data supplied to the object.

DATAFORMATAS: Sets whether data supplied to the object should be rendered as text or HTML.

dataPageSize: Sets or retrieves the number of records displayed in a table bound to a data source.

dataSrc: Sets or retrieves the source of the data for data binding.

DATASRC: Sets the source of the data for data binding. **dateTime**: Sets or retrieves the date and time of a modification to the object.

declare: Sets or retrieves a character string that can be used to implement your own declare functionality for the object.

defaultCharset: Retrieves the default character set from the current regional language settings.

defaultChecked: Sets or retrieves the state of the check box or radio button.

defaultSelected: Sets or retrieves the status of the option.

defaultStatus: Sets or retrieves the default message displayed in the status bar at the bottom of the window.

defaultValue: Sets or retrieves the initial contents of the object.

defer: Sets or retrieves the status of the script.

designMode: Sets or retrieves a value that indicates whether the document can be edited.

deviceXDPI: Retrieves the actual number of horizontal dots per inch (DPI) of the system's screen.

deviceYDPI: Retrieves the actual number of vertical dots per inch (DPI) of the system's screen.

dialogArguments: Retrieves the variable or array of variables passed into the modal dialog window.

dialogHeight: Sets or retrieves the height of the modal dialog window.

dialogLeft: Sets or retrieves the left coordinate of the modal dialog window.

dialogTop: Sets or retrieves the top coordinate of the modal dialog window.

dialogWidth: Sets or retrieves the width of the modal dialog window.

dir: Sets or retrieves the reading order of the object.

dir: Sets or retrieves a value that indicates the reading order of the object.

direction: Sets or retrieves the direction in which the text should scroll.

direction: Sets or retrieves the reading order of the object.

disabled: Sets or retrieves a value that you can use to implement your own disabled functionality for the object.

disabled: Sets or retrieves the value that indicates whether the user can interact with the object.

disabled: Sets or retrieves the status of the object.

disabled: Sets or retrieves whether a style sheet is applied to the object.

display: Sets or retrieves whether the object is rendered.

doctype: Retrieves the document type declaration associated with the current document.

document: Retrieves the HTML **document** in a given popup window.

documentElement: Retrieves a reference to the root node of the document.

domain: Sets or retrieves the security domain of the document.

dropEffect: Sets or retrieves the type of drag-and-drop operation and the type of cursor to display.

dynsrc: Sets or retrieves the address of a video clip or VRML world to display in the window.

effectAllowed: Sets or retrieves, on the source element, which data transfer operations are allowed for the object.

encoding: Sets or retrieves the MIME encoding for the form.

enctype: Sets or retrieves the Multipurpose Internet Mail Extensions (MIME) encoding for the form.

event: Sets or retrieves the event for which the script is written.

expando: Sets or retrieves a value indicating whether arbitrary variables can be created within the object.

face: Sets or retrieves the current typeface family.

fgColor: Sets or retrieves the foreground (text) color of the document.

FieldDelim: Specifies the character used to mark the end of data fields.

fileCreatedDate: Retrieves the date the file was created.

fileModifiedDate: Retrieves the date the file was last modified.

fileSize: Retrieves the file size.

fileUpdatedDate: Retrieves the date the file was last updated.

filter: Sets or retrieves the filter or collection of filters applied to the object.

firstChild: Retrieves a reference to the first child in the childNodes collection of the object.

font: Sets or retrieves a combination of separate font properties of the object. Alternatively, sets or retrieves one or more of six user-preference fonts.

fontFamily: Sets or retrieves the name of the font used for text in the object.

fontSize: Sets or retrieves a value that indicates the font size used for text in the object.

fontSmoothingEnabled: Retrieves whether the user has enabled font smoothing in the Display control panel.

fontStyle: Sets or retrieves the font style of the object as italic, normal, or oblique.

fontVariant: Sets or retrieves whether the text of the object is in small capital letters.

fontWeight: Sets or retrieves the numeric weight of the font of the object.

fontWeight: Sets or retrieves the weight of the font of the object.

form: Retrieves a reference to the form that the object is embedded in.

frame: Sets or retrieves the way the border frame around the table is displayed.

frameBorder: Sets or retrieves whether to display a border for the frame.

frameElement: Retrieves the frame or iframe object that is hosting the window in the parent document.

frameSpacing: Sets or retrieves the amount of additional space between the frames.

fromElement: Sets or retrieves the object from which activation or the mouse pointer is exiting during the event.

galleryImg: Sets or retrieves whether the My Pictures image toolbar is visible for the current image.

hash: Sets or retrieves the subsection of the href property that follows the number sign (#).

hasLayout: Retrieves a value that indicates whether the object has layout.

headers: Sets or retrieves a list of header cells that provide information for the object.

height: Retrieves the vertical resolution of the screen.

height: Sets or retrieves the height of the object.

height: Sets or retrieves the height of the object.

hidden: Sets or retrieves the value indicating whether the embedded object is invisible.

hideFocus: Sets or retrieves the value indicating whether the object visibly indicates that it has focus.

host: Sets or retrieves the hostname and port number of the location or URL.

hostname: Sets or retrieves the host name part of the location or URL.

href: Sets or retrieves the baseline URL on which relative links will be based.

href: Sets or retrieves the entire URL as a string.

href: Sets or retrieves the URL of the linked style sheet.

href: Sets or retrieves the destination URL or anchor point.

hreflang: Sets or retrieves the language code of the object.

hspace: Sets or retrieves the horizontal margin for the object.

htmlFor: Sets or retrieves the object to which the given label object is assigned.

htmlFor: Sets or retrieves the object that is bound to the event script.

htmlText: Retrieves the HTML source as a valid HTML fragment.

httpEquiv: Sets or retrieves information used to bind the META tag's content to an HTTP response header.

id: Retrieves the string identifying the object.

imeMode: Sets or retrieves the state of an Input Method Editor (IME).

implementation: Retrieves the implementation object of the current **document**.

indeterminate: Sets or retrieves whether the user has changed the status of a check box.

index: Sets or retrieves the ordinal position of an option in a list box.

innerHTML: Sets or retrieves the HTML between the start and end tags of the object.

innerText: Sets or retrieves the text between the start and end tags of the object.

isContentEditable: Retrieves the value indicating whether the user can edit the contents of the object.

isDisabled: Retrieves the value indicating whether the user can interact with the object.

isMap: Sets or retrieves whether the image is a server-side image map.

isMultiLine: Retrieves the value indicating whether the content of the object contains one or more lines.

isOpen: Retrieves a value indicating whether the popup window is open.

isTextEdit: Retrieves whether a TextRange object can be created using the object.

keyCode: Sets or retrieves the Unicode key code associated with the key that caused the event.

label: Sets or retrieves the label for the option group.

label: Sets or retrieves a value that you can use to implement your own label functionality for the object.

lang: Sets or retrieves the language to use.

language: Sets or retrieves the language in which the current script is written.

lastChild: Retrieves a reference to the last child in the childNodes collection of an object.

lastModified: Retrieves the date the page was last modified, if the page supplies one.

layoutFlow: Sets or retrieves the direction and flow of the content in the object.

layoutGrid: Sets or retrieves the composite document grid properties that specify the layout of text characters.

layoutGridChar: Sets or retrieves the size of the character grid used for rendering the text content of an element.

layoutGridLine: Sets or retrieves the gridline value used for rendering the text content of an element.

layoutGridMode: Sets or retrieves whether the text layout grid uses two dimensions.

layoutGridType: Sets or retrieves the type of grid used for rendering the text content of an element.

left: Sets or retrieves the position of the object relative to the left edge of the next positioned object in the document hierarchy.

left: Sets or retrieves the left coordinate of the rectangle surrounding the object content.

leftMargin: Sets or retrieves the left margin for the entire body of the page, overriding the default margin.

length: Retrieves the number of characters in a TextNode object.

length: Retrieves the number of elements in the History list.

length: Sets or retrieves the number of objects in a collection.

letterSpacing: Sets or retrieves the amount of additional space between letters in the object.

lineBreak: Sets or retrieves line-breaking rules for Japanese text.

lineHeight: Sets or retrieves the distance between lines in the object.

link: Sets or retrieves the color of the document links for the object.

linkColor: Sets or retrieves the color of the document links.

listStyle: Sets or retrieves up to three separate listStyle properties of the object.

listStyleImage: Sets or retrieves a value that indicates which image to use as a list-item marker for the object.

listStylePosition: Sets or retrieves a variable that indicates how the list-item marker is drawn relative to the content of the object.

listStyleType: Sets or retrieves the predefined type of the line-item marker for the object.

logicalXDPI: Retrieves the normal number of horizontal dots per inch (DPI) of the system's screen.

logicalYDPI: Retrieves the normal number of vertical dots per inch (DPI) of the system's screen.

longDesc: Sets or retrieves a Uniform Resource Identifier (URI) to a long description of the object.

loop: Sets or retrieves the number of times a marquee will play.

loop: Sets or retrieves the number of times a sound or video clip will loop when activated.

lowsrc: Sets or retrieves a lower resolution image to display.

margin: Sets or retrieves the width of the top, right, bottom, and left margins of the object.

marginBottom: Sets or retrieves the height of the bottom margin of the object.

marginHeight: Sets or retrieves the top and bottom margin heights before displaying the text in a frame.

marginLeft: Sets or retrieves the width of the left margin of the object.

marginRight: Sets or retrieves the width of the right margin of the object.

marginTop: Sets or retrieves the height of the top margin of the object.

marginWidth: Sets or retrieves the left and right margin widths before displaying the text in a frame.

maxHeight: Sets or retrieves the maximum height for displayable block level elements.

maxLength: Sets or retrieves the maximum number of characters that the user can enter in a text control.

maxWidth: Sets or retrieves the maximum width for displayable block level elements.

media: Sets or retrieves the media type.

menuArguments: Returns the window object where the context menu item was executed.

method: Sets or retrieves how to send the form data to the server.

Methods: Sets or retrieves the list of HTTP methods supported by the object.

minHeight: Sets or retrieves the minimum height for an element.

minHeight: Sets or retrieves the minimum height for displayable block level elements.

minWidth: Sets or retrieves the minimum width for displayable block level element.

msInterpolationMode: Sets or retrieves the interpolation (resampling) method used to stretch images.

multiple: Sets or retrieves the Boolean value indicating whether multiple items can be selected from a list.

name: Sets or retrieves the value specified in the CONTENT attribute of the meta object.

name: Retrieves the name of the namespace.

name: Sets or retrieves the name of an input parameter for an element.

name: Sets or retrieves the frame name.

name: Sets or retrieves the name of the object.

name: Sets or retrieves a value that indicates the window name.

nameProp: Retrieves the file name specified in the href or src property of the object.

nextPage: Retrieves the position of the next page within a print template.

nextSibling: Retrieves a reference to the next child of the parent for the object.

nodeName: Retrieves the name of a particular type of node.

nodeType: Retrieves the type of the requested node.

nodeValue: Sets or retrieves the value of a node.

noHref: Sets or retrieves whether clicks in this region cause action.

noResize: Sets or retrieves whether the user can resize the frame.

noShade: Sets or retrieves whether the horizontal rule is drawn with 3-D shading.

noWrap: Sets or retrieves whether the browser automatically performs wordwrap.

object: Retrieves the contained object.

offscreenBuffering: Sets or retrieves whether objects are drawn offscreen before being made visible to the user.

offsetHeight: Retrieves the height of the object relative to the layout or coordinate parent, as specified by the offsetParent property.

offsetLeft: Retrieves the calculated left position of the object relative to the layout or coordinate parent, as specified by the **offsetParent** property.

offsetParent: Retrieves a reference to the container object that defines the offsetTop and offsetLeft properties of the object.

offsetTop: Retrieves the calculated top position of the object relative to the layout or coordinate parent, as specified by the **offsetParent** property.

offsetWidth: Retrieves the width of the object relative to the layout or coordinate parent, as specified by the offsetParent property.

offsetX: Sets or retrieves the x-coordinate of the mouse pointer's position relative to the object firing the event.

offsetY: Sets or retrieves the y-coordinate of the mouse pointer's position relative to the object firing the event.

onLine: Retrieves a value indicating whether the system is in global offline mode.

onreadystatechange: Sets the event handler for asynchronous requests.

opener: Sets or retrieves a reference to the window that created the current window.

outerHTML: Sets or retrieves the object and its content in HTML.

outerText: Sets or retrieves the text of the object.

overflow: Sets or retrieves a value indicating how to manage the content of the object when the content exceeds the height or width of the object.

overflowX: Sets or retrieves how to manage the content of the object when the content exceeds the width of the object.

overflowY: Sets or retrieves how to manage the content of the object when the content exceeds the height of the object.

ownerDocument: Retrieves the document object associated with the node.

owningElement: Retrieves the next object in the HTML hierarchy.

padding: Sets or retrieves the amount of space to insert between the object and its margin or, if there is a border, between the object and its border.

paddingBottom: Sets or retrieves the amount of space to insert between the bottom border of the object and the content.

paddingLeft: Sets or retrieves the amount of space to insert between the left border of the object and the content.

paddingRight: Sets or retrieves the amount of space to insert between the right border of the object and the content.

paddingTop: Sets or retrieves the amount of space to insert between the top border of the object and the content.

pageBreakAfter: Sets or retrieves a value indicating whether a page break occurs after the object.

pageBreakBefore: Sets or retrieves a string indicating whether a page break occurs before the object.

palette: Retrieves the palette used for the embedded document.

parent: Retrieves the parent of the window in the object hierarchy.

parentElement: Retrieves the parent object in the object hierarchy.

parentNode: Retrieves the parent object in the document hierarchy.

parentStyleSheet: Retrieves the style sheet that imported the current style sheets.

parentTextEdit: Retrieves the container object in the document hierarchy that can be used to create a TextRange containing the original object.

parentWindow: Retrieves a reference to the container object of the window.

pathname: Sets or retrieves the file name or path specified by the object.

pixelBottom: Sets or retrieves the bottom position of the object.

pixelHeight: Sets or retrieves the height of the object.

pixelLeft: Sets or retrieves the left position of the object.

pixelRight: Sets or retrieves the right position of the object.

pixelTop: Sets or retrieves the top position of the object.

pixelWidth: Sets or retrieves the width of the object.

platform: Retrieves the name of the user's operating system.

pluginspage: Retrieves the URL of the plug-in used to view an embedded document.

port: Sets or retrieves the port number associated with a URL.

posBottom: Sets or retrieves the bottom position of the object in the units specified by the bottom attribute.

posHeight: Sets or retrieves the height of the object in the units specified by the height attribute.

position: Sets or retrieves the type of positioning used for the object.

posLeft: Sets or retrieves the left position of the object in the units specified by the left attribute.

posRight: Sets or retrieves the right position of the object in the units specified by the right attribute.

posTop: Sets or retrieves the top position of the object in the units specified by the top attribute.

posWidth: Sets or retrieves the width of the object in the units specified by the width attribute.

previousSibling: Retrieves a reference to the previous child of the parent for the object.

profile: Sets or retrieves one or more URI(s) in which the object's properties and legal values for those properties are defined.

propertyName: Sets or retrieves the name of the property that changes on the object.

protocol: Sets or retrieves the protocol portion of a URL.

pseudoClass: Retrieves a string that identifies the pseudo class of the page or pages an @page rule applies to.

qualifier: Sets or retrieves the name of the data member provided by a data source object.

readOnly: Retrieves whether the rule or style sheet is defined on the page or is imported.

readOnly: Sets or retrieves the value indicated whether the content of the object is read-only.

readyState: Retrieves the current state of the request operation.

readyState: Retrieves the current state of the object.

readyState: Retrieves a value that indicates the current state of the object.

readyState: Retrieves the current state of the object.

reason: Sets or retrieves the result of the data transfer for a data source object.

recordNumber: Retrieves the ordinal record from the data set that generated the object.

recordset: Sets or retrieves from a data source object a reference to the default record set.

referrer: Retrieves the URL of the location that referred the user to the current page.
rel: Sets or retrieves the relationship between the object and the destination of the link.

repeat: Retrieves whether the onkeydown event is being repeated.

responseBody: Retrieves the response body as an array of unsigned bytes.

responseText: Retrieves the response body as a string.

responseXML: Retrieves the response body as an Extensible Markup Language (XML) Document Object Model (DOM) object.

returnValue: Sets or retrieves the value returned from the modal dialog window.

returnValue: Sets or retrieves the return value from the event.

rev: Sets or retrieves the relationship between the object and the destination of the link.

right: Sets or retrieves the right coordinate of the rectangle surrounding the object content.

right: Sets or retrieves the position of the object relative to the right edge of the next positioned object in the document hierarchy.

rightMargin: Sets or retrieves the right margin for the entire body of the page.

rowIndex: Retrieves the position of the object in the rows collection for the **table**.

rows: Sets or retrieves the frame heights of the object.

rows: Sets or retrieves the number of horizontal rows contained in the object.

rowSpan: Sets or retrieves how many rows in a table the cell should span.

rubyAlign: Sets or retrieves the position of the ruby text specified by the rt object.

rubyOverhang: Sets or retrieves the position of the ruby text specified by the rt object.

rubyPosition: Sets or retrieves the position of the ruby text specified by the rt object.

rules: Sets or retrieves which dividing lines (inner borders) are displayed.

saveType: Retrieves the clipboard type when oncontentsave fires.

scheme: Sets or retrieves a scheme to be used in interpreting the value of a property specified for the object.

scope: Sets or retrieves the group of cells in a table to which the object's information applies.

scopeName: Retrieves the namespace defined for the element.

screenLeft: Retrieves the x-coordinate of the upper left-hand corner of the browser's client area, relative to the upper left-hand corner of the screen.

screenTop: Retrieves the y-coordinate of the top corner of the browser's client area, relative to the top corner of the screen.

screenX: Retrieves the x-coordinate of the mouse pointer's position relative to the user's screen.

screenY: Sets or retrieves the y-coordinate of the mouse pointer's position relative to the user's screen.

scroll: Sets or retrieves a value that indicates whether the scroll bars are turned on or off.

scrollAmount: Sets or retrieves the number of pixels the text scrolls between each subsequent drawing of the marquee.

scrollbar3dLightColor: Sets or retrieves the color of the top and left edges of the scroll box and scroll arrows of a scroll bar.

scrollbarArrowColor: Sets or retrieves the color of the arrow elements of a scroll arrow.

scrollbarBaseColor: Sets or retrieves the color of the main elements of a scroll bar, which include the scroll box, track, and scroll arrows.

scrollbarDarkShadowColor: Sets or retrieves the color of the gutter of a scroll bar.

scrollbarFaceColor: Sets or retrieves the color of the scroll box and scroll arrows of a scroll bar.

scrollbarHighlightColor: Sets or retrieves the color of the top and left edges of the scroll box and scroll arrows of a scroll bar.

scrollbarShadowColor: Sets or retrieves the color of the bottom and right edges of the scroll box and scroll arrows of a scroll bar.

scrollbarTrackColor: Sets or retrieves the color of the track element of a scroll bar.

scrollDelay: Sets or retrieves the speed of the marquee scroll.

scrollHeight: Retrieves the scrolling height of the object.

scrolling: Sets or retrieves whether the frame can be scrolled.

scrollLeft: Sets or retrieves the distance between the left edge of the object and the leftmost portion of the content currently visible in the window.

scrollTop: Sets or retrieves the distance between the top of the object and the topmost portion of the content currently visible in the window.

scrollWidth: Retrieves the scrolling width of the object.

search: Sets or retrieves the substring of the href property that follows the question mark.

sectionRowIndex: Retrieves the position of the object in the tBody, tHead, tFoot, or **rows** collection.

SECURITY: Sets the value indicating whether the source file of a frame or iframe has specific security restrictions applied.

selected: Sets or retrieves whether the option in the list box is the default item.

selectedIndex: Sets or retrieves the index of the selected option in a select object.

selector: Retrieves a string that identifies which page or pages an @page rule applies to.

selectorText: Retrieves a string that identifies which elements the corresponding style sheet rule applies to.

self: Retrieves a reference to the current window or frame.

shape: Sets or retrieves the shape of the object.

shiftKey: Sets or retrieves the state of the SHIFT key.

shiftLeft: Retrieves the state of the left SHIFT key.

size: Sets or retrieves the height of the hr object.

size: Sets or retrieves the number of rows in the list box.

size: Sets or retrieves the font size of the object.

size: Sets or retrieves the size of the control.

sourceIndex: Retrieves the ordinal position of the object, in source order, as the object appears in the document's all collection.

span: Sets or retrieves the number of columns in the group.

specified: Retrieves whether an attribute has been specified.

src: Sets or retrieves the URL of a sound to play.

src: Retrieves the URL to an external file that contains the source code or data.

src: Sets or retrieves a URL to be loaded by the object.

srcElement: Sets or retrieves the object that fired the event.

srcFilter: Sets or retrieves the filter object that caused the onfilterchange event to fire.

srcUrn: Retrieves the Uniform Resource Name (URN) of the behavior that fired the event.

standby: Sets or retrieves a message to be displayed while an object is loading.

start: Sets or retrieves the starting number for an ordered list.

start: Sets or retrieves when a video clip file should begin playing.

status: Sets or retrieves the message in the status bar at the bottom of the window.

status: Retrieves the HTTP status code of the request.

status: Sets or retrieves the value indicating whether the control is selected.

statusText: Retrieves the friendly HTTP status of the request.

STYLE: Sets an inline style for the element.

styleFloat: Sets or retrieves on which side of the object the text will flow.

summary: Sets or retrieves a description and/or structure of the object.

systemLanguage: Retrieves the default language used by the operating system.

tabIndex: Sets or retrieves the index that defines the tab order for the object.

tableLayout: Sets or retrieves a string that indicates whether the table layout is fixed.

tabStop: Sets or retrieves whether an element behavior can receive focus and participate in the tabbing sequence.

tagName: Retrieves the tag name of the object.

tagUrn: Sets or retrieves the URN specified in the namespace declaration.

target: Sets or retrieves the window or frame at which to target content.

text: Sets or retrieves the text (foreground) color for the document body.

text: Sets or retrieves the text string specified by the option tag.

text: Sets or retrieves the text contained within the range.

text: Retrieves or sets the text of the object as a string.

textAlign: Sets or retrieves whether the text in the object is left-aligned, right-aligned, centered, or justified.

textAlignLast: Sets or retrieves how to align the last line or only line of text in the object.

textAutospace: Sets or retrieves the autospacing and narrow space width adjustment of text.

textDecoration: Sets or retrieves a value that indicates whether the text in the object has blink, line-through, overline, or underline decorations.

textDecorationBlink: Sets or retrieves a Boolean value that indicates whether the object's textDecoration property has a value of "blink."

textDecorationLineThrough: Sets or retrieves a Boolean value indicating whether the text in the object has a line drawn through it.

textDecorationNone: Sets or retrieves the Boolean value indicating whether the textDecoration property for the object has been set to none.

textDecorationOverline: Sets or retrieves a Boolean value indicating whether the text in the object has a line drawn over it.

textDecorationUnderline: Sets or retrieves whether the text in the object is underlined.

textIndent: Sets or retrieves the indentation of the first line of text in the object.

textJustify: Sets or retrieves the type of alignment used to justify text in the object.

textKashidaSpace: Sets or retrieves the ratio of kashida expansion to white space expansion when justifying lines of text in the object.

textOverflow: Sets or retrieves a value that indicates whether to render ellipses(...) to indicate text overflow.

textTransform: Sets or retrieves the rendering of the text in the object.

textUnderlinePosition: Sets or retrieves the position of the underline decoration that is set through the textDecoration property of the object.

tFoot: Retrieves the tFoot object of the table.

tHead: Retrieves the tHead object of the table.

title: Sets or retrieves advisory information (a ToolTip) for the object.

title: Sets or retrieves the title of the style sheet.

toElement: Sets or retrieves a reference to the object toward which the user is moving the mouse pointer.

top: Sets or retrieves the position of the object relative to the top of the next positioned object in the document hierarchy.

top: Retrieves the topmost ancestor window.

top: Sets or retrieves the top coordinate of the rectangle surrounding the object content.

topMargin: Sets or retrieves the margin for the top of the page.

trueSpeed: Sets or retrieves whether the position of the marquee is calculated using the scrollDelay and scrollAmount properties and the actual time elapsed from the last clock tick.

type: Retrieves the classification and default behavior of the button.

type: Sets or retrieves the content type of the resource designated by the value attribute.

type: Sets or retrieves the MIME type for the associated scripting engine.

type: Retrieves the type of selection.

type: Retrieves the Cascading Style Sheets (CSS) language in which the style sheet is written.

type: Retrieves the CSS language in which the style sheet is written.

type: Retrieves the type of control.

type: Sets or retrieves the style of the list.

type: Sets or retrieves the event name from the event object.

type: Sets or retrieves the MIME type of the object.

type: Retrieves or initially sets the type of input control represented by the object.

type: Retrieves the type of **select** control based on the value of the MULTIPLE attribute.

typeDetail: Retrieves the name of the selection type.

unicodeBidi: Sets or retrieves the level of embedding with respect to the bidirectional algorithm.

uniqueID: Retrieves an autogenerated, unique identifier for the object.

units: Sets or retrieves the height and width units of the embed object.

UNSELECTABLE: Specifies that an element cannot be selected.

updateInterval: Sets or retrieves the update interval for the screen.

URL: Sets or retrieves the URL for the current document.

URLUnencoded: Retrieves the URL for the document, stripped of any character encoding.

urn: Sets or retrieves a URN for a target document.

useMap: Sets or retrieves the URL, often with a bookmark extension (#name), to use as a client-side image map.

userAgent: Retrieves a string equivalent to the HTTP user-agent request header.

userLanguage: Retrieves the operating system's natural language setting.

vAlign: Sets or retrieves whether the caption appears at the top or bottom of the table.

vAlign: Sets or retrieves how text and other content are vertically aligned within the object that contains them.

value: Sets or retrieves the value of the object.

value: Retrieves the file name of the input object after the text is set by user input.

value: Sets or retrieves the displayed value for the control object. This value is returned to the server when the control object is submitted.

value: Sets or retrieves the value of a list item.

value: Sets or retrieves the value of an input parameter for an element.

value: Retrieves or sets the text in the entry field of the textArea element.

value: Sets or retrieves the default or selected value of the control.

value: Sets or retrieves the value which is returned to the server when the form control is submitted.

valueType: Sets or retrieves the data type of the value attribute.

vcard_name: Sets or retrieves the vCard value of the object to use for the AutoComplete box.

version: Sets or retrieves the Document Type Definition (DTD) version that governs the current document.

verticalAlign: Sets or retrieves the vertical alignment of the object.

viewInheritStyle: Sets or retrieves a value that indicates whether the document fragment inherits the CSS styles set in the primary document.

viewLink: Sets or retrieves the document object that supplies content to the master element.

viewMasterTab: Sets or retrieves a value that indicates whether the master element of a viewlink is included in the tab sequence of the primary document.

visibility: Sets or retrieves whether the content of the object is displayed.

vLink: Sets or retrieves the color of links in the object that have already been visited.

vlinkColor: Sets or retrieves the color of the links that the user has visited.

volume: Sets or retrieves the volume setting for the sound.

vspace: Sets or retrieves the vertical margin for the object.

wheelDelta: Retrieves the distance and direction the wheel button has rolled.

whiteSpace: Sets or retrieves a value that indicates whether lines are automatically broken inside the object.

width: Sets or retrieves a value that you can use to implement your own width functionality for the object.

width: Retrieves the horizontal resolution of the screen.

width: Sets or retrieves the calculated width of the object.

width: Sets or retrieves the width of the object.

width: Sets or retrieves the width of the object.

wordBreak: Sets or retrieves line-breaking behavior within words, particularly where multiple languages appear in the object.

wordSpacing: Sets or retrieves the amount of additional space between words in the object.

wordWrap: Sets or retrieves whether to break words when the content exceeds the boundaries of its container.

wrap: Sets or retrieves how to handle wordwrapping in the object.

writingMode: Sets or retrieves the direction and flow of the content in the object.

x: Sets or retrieves the x-coordinate, in pixels, of the mouse pointer's position relative to a relatively positioned parent element.

XMLDocument: Retrieves a reference to the XML

XMLHttpRequest: Instantiates the XMLHttpRequest object for the window.

XMLNS: Declares a namespace for custom tags in an HTML document.

XSLDocument: Retrieves a reference to the top-level node of the Extensible Stylesheet Language (XSL) document.

y: Sets or retrieves the y-coordinate, in pixels, of the mouse pointer's position relative to a relatively positioned parent element.

zIndex: Sets or retrieves the stacking order of positioned objects.

zoom: Sets or retrieves the magnification scale of the object.

Question 100: Objects

Can you give me the list of the "objects" defined by DHTML?

A: The following is the list of objects:

a: Designates the start or destination of a hypertext link.

abbr: Inserts an abbreviation into an HTML page.

acronym: Indicates an acronym abbreviation.

address: Specifies information, such as address, signature, and authorship, of the current document.

applet: Places executable content on the page.

area: Defines the shape, coordinates, and associated URL of one hyperlink region within a client-side image map.

attribute: Represents an attribute or property of an HTML element as an object.

b: Specifies that the text should be rendered in bold.

base: Specifies an explicit URL used to resolve links and references to external sources such as images and style sheets.

baseFont: Sets a base font value to be used as the default font when rendering text.

bdo: Allows authors to disable the bidirectional algorithm for selected fragments of text.

bgSound: Enables an author to create pages with background sounds or soundtracks.

big: Specifies that the enclosed text should be displayed in a larger font than the current font.

blockQuote: Sets apart a quotation in text.

body: Specifies the beginning and end of the document body.

br: Inserts a line break.

button: Specifies a container for rich HTML that is rendered as a button.

caption: Specifies a brief description for a table.

center: Centers subsequent text and images.

cite: Indicates a citation by rendering text in italic.

clientInformation: Contains information about the browser.

clipboardData: Provides access to predefined clipboard formats for use in editing operations.

code: Specifies a code sample.

col: Specifies column-based defaults for the table properties.

colGroup: Specifies property defaults for a column or group of columns in a table.

comment: Indicates a comment that is not displayed.

currentStyle: Represents the cascaded format and style of the object as specified by global style sheets, inline styles, and HTML attributes.

custom: Represents a user-defined element.

dataTransfer: Provides access to predefined clipboard formats for use in drag-and-drop operations.

dd: Indicates the definition in a definition list. The definition is usually indented in the definition list.

defaults: Programmatically sets default properties on an element behavior.

del: Indicates text that has been deleted from the document.

dfn: Indicates the defining instance of a term.

Dialog Helper: Provides access the color dialog box, as well as the block format and fonts collections.

dir: Denotes a directory list.

div: Specifies a container that renders HTML.

dl: Denotes a definition list.

document: Represents the HTML document in a given browser window.

dt: Indicates a definition term within a definition list.

em: Emphasizes text, usually by rendering it in italic.

embed: Allows documents of any type to be embedded.

event: Represents the state of an event, such as the element in which the event occurred, the state of the keyboard keys, the location of the mouse, and the state of the mouse buttons.

external: Allows access to an additional object model provided by host applications of the Microsoft Internet Explorer browser components.

fieldSet: Draws a box around the text and other elements that the field set contains.

font: Specifies a new font, size, and color to be used for rendering the enclosed text.

form: Specifies that the contained controls take part in a form.

frame: Specifies an individual frame within a FRAMESET element.

frameSet: Specifies a frameset, which is used to organize multiple frames and nested framesets.

head: Provides an unordered collection of information about the document.

history: Contains information about the URLs visited by the client.

hn: Renders text in heading style.

hr: Draws a horizontal rule.

html: Identifies the document as containing HTML elements.

HTML Comment: Prevents any enclosed text or HTML source code from being parsed and displayed in the browser window.

i: Specifies that the text should be rendered in italic, where available.

iframe: Creates inline floating frames.

img: Embeds an image or a video clip in the document.

implementation: Contains information about the modules supported by the object.

IMPORT: Imports a tag definition from an element behavior.

input: Creates a variety of form input controls.

input type: button: Creates a button control.

input type: checkbox: Creates a check box control.

input type: file : Creates a file upload object with a text box and Browse button.

input type: hidden : Transmits state information about client/server interaction.

input type: image : Creates an image control that, when clicked, causes the form to be immediately submitted.

input type: password : Creates a single-line text entry control similar to the INPUT type: text control, except that text is not displayed as the user enters it.

input type: radio : Creates a radio button control.

input type: reset : Creates a button that, when clicked, resets the form's controls to their initial values.

input type: submit : Creates a button that, when clicked, submits the form.

input type: text : Creates a single-line text entry control.

ins : Specifies text that has been inserted into the document.

isIndex : Causes the browser to display a dialog window that prompts the user for a single line of input.

kbd: Renders text in a fixed-width font.

label: Specifies a label for another element on the page.

legend: Inserts a caption into the box drawn by the fieldSet object.

li: Denotes one item in a list.

link: Enables the current document to establish links to external documents.

listing: Renders text in a fixed-width font.

location: Contains information about the current URL.

map: Contains coordinate data for client-side image maps.

marquee: Creates a scrolling text marquee.

menu: Creates an unordered list of items.

meta: Conveys hidden information about the document to the server and the client.

namespace: Dynamically imports an element behavior into a document.

navigator: Contains information about the browser.

nextID: Creates unique identifiers that text editing software can read.

noBR: Renders text without line breaks.

noFrames: Contains HTML for browsers that do not support FRAMESET elements.

noScript: Specifies HTML to be displayed in browsers that do not support scripting.

object: Inserts an object into the HTML page.

ol: Draws lines of text as a numbered list.

optGroup: Allows authors to group choices logically in a select element.

option: Denotes one choice in a SELECT element.

p: Denotes a paragraph.

page: Represents an @page rule within a styleSheet.

param: Sets the initial value of a property for an APPLET, EMBED, or OBJECT element.

plainText: Not currently supported.

popup: A special type of overlapped window typically used for dialog boxes, message boxes, and other temporary windows that appear separate from an application's main window.

pre: Renders text in a fixed-width font.

q: Sets apart a quotation in text.

rt: Designates the ruby text for the RUBY element.

ruby: Designates an annotation or pronunciation guide to be placed above or inline with a string of text.

rule: Represents a style within a Cascading Style Sheets (CSS) that consists of a selector and one or more declarations.

runtimeStyle: Represents the cascaded format and style of the object that overrides the format and style specified in global style sheets, inline styles, and HTML attributes.

s: Renders text in strike-through type.

samp: Specifies a code sample.

screen: Contains information about the client's screen and rendering capabilities.

script: Specifies a script for the page that is interpreted by a script engine.

select: Denotes a list box or drop-down list.

selection: Represents the active selection, which is a highlighted block of text, and/or other elements in the document on which a user or a script can carry out some action.

small: Specifies that the enclosed text should be displayed in a smaller font.

span: Specifies an inline text container.

strike: Renders text in strike-through type.

strong: Renders text in bold.

style: Represents the current settings of all possible inline styles for a given element.

style: Specifies a style sheet for the page.

styleSheet: Represents a single style sheet in the document.

sub: Specifies that the enclosed text should be displayed in subscript, using a smaller font than the current font.

sup: Specifies that the enclosed text should be displayed in superscript, using a smaller font than the current font.

table: Specifies that the contained content is organized into a table with rows and columns.

tBody: Designates rows as the body of the table.

td: Specifies a cell in a table.

textArea: Specifies a multiline text input control.

TextNode: Represents a string of text as a node in the document hierarchy.

TextRange: Represents text in an HTML element.

TextRectangle: Specifies a rectangle that contains a line of text in either an element or a TextRange object.

tFoot: Designates rows as the table's footer.

th: Specifies a header column. Header columns are centered within the cell and are bold.

tHead: Designates rows as the table's header.

title: Contains the title of the document.

tr: Specifies a row in a table.

tt: Renders text in a fixed-width font.

u: Renders text that is underlined.

ul: Draws lines of text as a bulleted list.

userProfile: Provides methods that allow a script to request read access to and perform read actions on a user's profile information.

var: Defines a programming variable. Typically renders in an italic font style.

wbr: Inserts a soft line break into a block of NOBR text.

window: Represents an open window in the browser.

xml: Defines an XML data island on an HTML page.

XMLHttpRequest: Represents a Extensible Markup Language (XML) request via HTTP.

xmp: Renders text used for examples in a fixed-width font.

ACKNOWLEDGEMENTS

http://www.dhtmlshock.com/faqs.asp

http://www.dhtmlshock.com/forum/topic.asp?TOPIC_ID: 3593

http://msdn.microsoft.com/workshop/author/dhtml/reference/dhtml_reference_entry.asp

http://en.wikipedia.org/wiki/Cascading_Style_Sheets

http://en.wikipedia.org/wiki/HTML

http://en.wikipedia.org/wiki/DHTML

http://www.tek-tips.com/threadminder.cfm?pid: 215

http://wdvl.internet.com/WDVL/Forum/css.html

http://forums.aspfree.com/html-javascript-and-css-help-7/

Index

www.ingramcontent.com/pod-product-compliance
Lightning Source LLC
LaVergne TN
LVHW042331060326
832902LV00006B/111